DESTINATION: COMMUNITY

SMALL-GROUP
MINISTRY MANUAL

BY RICK HOWERTON WITH BEN COLTER

"IN DESTINATION: COMMUNITY, Rick spreads out a fresh canvas for envisioning small-group ministry. While it provides everything you need to launch and cultivate a small-group ministry or lead an individual small group, it reaches beyond the how-to's into the heart and soul of living in community. Whether you're a veteran small-group leader or just starting the journey, this book will challenge and equip you to do life together and not just play at church. This roadmap for the small-group journey is a great tool for leaders who are serious about experiencing more of what God desires—redemptive, culture-transforming community!"

—**Steve Gladen**, Pastor of the Small-Group Community, Saddleback Church

"DESTINATION: COMMUNITY lays out a detailed picture of what biblical community is, and what it is not. Rick Howerton will inspire you with stories from the heart of small-group life and equip you with the processes that make small-group community happen organically without highly programmed or forced strategies. Destination: Community gives a refreshing perspective on truly redemptive community."

—**Dan Lentz**, Director, SmallGroups.com

"BEING A VORACIOUS small-group leadership book reader, I found Destination: Community to be an excellent source of practical information. Rick shares key principles with personal stories and drew me into the book with his easygoing and engaging writing style. You'll enjoy reading this book, and reap many rewards by applying the content to your small group!"

—**Randall Neighbour**, Author, Small-Group Consultant, President, TOUCH® Outreach Ministries

THIS BOOK IS DEDICATED TO JULIE ...

My anonymous confidante,
My courageous corrector, my portrait of grace,
My co-leader and co-laborer,

My best friend, my favorite gift ever, my wife.

NO BOOK IS WRITTEN IN A VACUUM. Any honest author acknowledges that the real experts, the founding fathers in a given area of study, have come before him and established a philosophical foundation for the work he is doing. And any reflective author is vividly aware that there have been individuals God has placed along the path that have shaped him, taught him, and influenced the ideas that flow from his heart to his fingers and onto the page. And a wise man realizes that he is not capable of crossing all the t's and dotting all the i's himself, that gifted editors, graphic designers, and a visionary publisher stimulate sedentary words until they dance gracefully into the soul of the reader.

AND SO, I WANT TO ACKNOWLEDGE ...

Lyman Coleman and Bill Donahue—giants on whose shoulders the small-group movement has been carried and greatly influenced for decades; men whose work and lives have inspired myself and thousands of others.

The Kentucky Baptist Campus Ministry family of 1984 through 1993 and the Living Hope Baptist Church staff of 1993 through 2000. Thanks for helping me take my first steps toward authenticity and Christian community.

The present Serendipity House team, a group of discoverers destined to journey together.

The Bridge ... My family, my friends, my passion, the church on the journey.

Contributing writers: Josh Howerton, one of my great sons who provided the section on Youth Small Groups, and Ben Colter, who provided various elements throughout the book.

And those who have taken an incoherent manuscript and transformed it into an intelligible and powerful book: Ben Colter and Lori Mayes, editors extraordinaire; Stacey "Hawkeye" Owens and Jenna Anderson, proofers; Micah Kandros, a gifted graphics designer; Brian Marschall, one of the most fun and certainly one of the best art directors in the land; and Ron Keck, the leader of the Serendipity House team, a man whose life and uncompromising passion have strengthened the company and transformed all of us who are Serendipity House today.

CONTENTS

DESTINATION:COMMUNITY

CONTENTS

NOTE: Be sure to check out the downloadable bonus material, tip sheets, and helpful small-group forms in the Group Tools section on the Web at www.Serendipity House.com/Community.

DESTINATION OR DETOUR?

IF YOUR DESTINATION IS COMMUNITY, then small-group ministry is the vehicle to take you there. We at Serendipity House like to define an effective, biblically-driven small group as "a group of people unwilling to settle for anything less than redemptive community." Yet, even that description doesn't fully explain what a heart-pounding, courage-creating, and life-transforming ride such a group can experience. The very act of authentically living the Christian life together while passionately pursuing healing, wholeness, and heart awakening will cause group members to realize that even though life is messy, God loves working in and through our messiness.

DUCT TAPE WHEN LIFE IS FALLING APART

Life in community with other Christ-followers in an authentic, accepting, and relationally connected small group is God's design for every person. Healthy, effective small groups provide each member duct tape when life is falling apart, fireworks in times of celebration, embers of desire when life grows cold and indifferent, and huddles that end the lonely game of living in isolation.

So, why aren't vibrant, redemptive small groups the norm? In my years as a small-group pastor, consultant, and senior pastor, I have seen many people and churches believe that all the descriptors mentioned above should, can, and will happen in small groups, but they've become disappointed and disillusioned by less-than-impressive experiences. Consequently, they've chosen to disengage from the whole small-group journey.

EMBERS OF DESIRE WHEN LIFE GROWS COLD
FIREWORKS IN TIMES OF CELEBRATION

What went wrong? In most of the churches I've worked with, at least one of the following detours is responsible for the frustrating results:

✳ DETOUR 1:

Primary principles and practices of small-group life are not established.

If you're a golfer, you understand the importance of lining up your putt to perfection. It's called "getting the right line." You may spend five or six minutes determining the line for your putt because once the ball is rolling, it's either going to hit the hole or it's not. And, if you miss, you're going to experience frustration, even defeat. Many small-group leaders and churches have grown frustrated with the small-group concept when the truth is they didn't line up their shot so the ball would drop into the hole. Getting the right principles and practices established is how you line up your shot. If the correct principles and practices are not instilled in leaders at all levels, then each individual leader will fill that philosophical chasm with his or her own ideas and beliefs.

✳ DETOUR 2:

The leader is unable to separate from past paradigms and completely embrace small-group life.

A small-group leader once said, "I want to be a great small-group leader but I keep finding myself teaching a Sunday School class at my house on Tuesday night." Many small-group leaders have led groups in Adult Education classes, 12-Step programs, or Adult Bible Fellowships and feel comfortable doing what they've done in the past. These leaders are excited about their groups, but their attendees feel they've been duped because their expectations don't materialize. There is an important place for teaching, but it's not teaching that will carry a group down the road to community. Successful small-group leaders must shed their old paradigms and comfortable formats in order to fully embrace the principles and practices of small-group life.

SHED COMFORTABLE PARADIGMS FULLY EMBRACE SMALL-GROUP LIFE

✳ DETOUR 3:

The church expects results too quickly from the small-group ministry.

It's impossible for something to mature faster than its predetermined rate of growth. However, many churches expect a small-group ministry to develop mature disciples in just a few months. This is like asking a 25-year-old woman to give birth to a baby and, in two months, make sure that child looks, acts, and reproduces like a 25-year-old woman. It's impossible! Poet Juan Ramon Jimenez wrote, "The great assassin of life is haste, the desire to reach things before the right time ...." [1] Building a foundation for a small-group ministry is all about developing people, and that takes time.

✳ DETOUR 4:

The small-group ministry lacks a passionate, Spirit-led leader.

Regarding small-group leadership, Bill Hybels once offered the following challenge: "Either pull the leadership trigger or give the gun away." He is passionate about courageous leadership because, as his close friend John Maxwell explains, "Everything rises and falls on leadership." The individual spearheading a small-group ministry must lead! He or she must be entrepreneurial, organizationally minded, strategy driven, and unapologetically passionate about people. At the same time the overall ministry leader must be able to create a blueprint for the ministry, develop a ministry team, instill vision, build the ministry, and rebuild it if necessary while the vehicle is in motion. Many churches try unsuccessfully to launch a small-group ministry by handing the keys to a gifted teacher, faithful officer, or skilled administrator. Too often, without the right leadership, the ministry takes a wrong turn before the key is even in the ignition. John Maxwell is right; everything does rise and fall on leadership. Too many small-group ministries have fallen into oblivion because of the lack of a passionate pastoral leader with the spiritual gift of leadership who is willing to roll up his or her shirtsleeves and get to work.

ENTREPENEURIAL
STRATEGY DRIVEN
PASSIONATE ABOUT PEOPLE

✳ DETOUR 5:

The church believes curriculum is the key to life-changing small groups.

When church leaders believe discipleship is based primarily on proposition rather than relationships and experiencing God, they trust a curriculum to drive the spiritual formation of their members. Propositionally based discipleship is built around the belief that the more knowledge an individual has, the deeper the level of spiritual growth he or she will experience. When the gathering of information is seen as an end in itself, the small group becomes just another Bible study. But, Jesus modeled a relationally based discipleship. In His discipleship model, group members learn from relationships with others who are on their own journeys toward spiritual maturity. Small-group curriculum must be seen for what it is—a tool in the toolkit. Effective small-group material, like the Serendipity House line of products, will help group members gain biblical knowledge and facilitate experiences that are transformational. Effective material will also be a conversation starter that invites each person to share his or her story and hear the stories of others.

JESUS DISCIPLED RELATIONALLY

✳ DETOUR 6:

The ministry is based on an organizational rather than an organic approach.

Realizing that small groups are organic is essential to the growth of any small-group ministry. According to "The Open Door Website," (www.knockonthedoor.com) there are seven characteristics that define an organism:

⊝ **FEEDING** - All living organisms need substances from their environment to obtain energy, grow, and stay healthy.

⊝ **MOVEMENT** - All living organisms show movement of one kind or another (internal and external).

⊝ **BREATHING OR RESPIRATION** - All living things exchange gases with their environment.

⊝ **EXCRETION** - Excretion is the removal of waste from the body. If this waste was allowed to remain in the body, it could be poisonous. All living things need to eliminate waste from their bodies.

⊝ **GROWTH** - When living things feed, they gain energy. Some of this energy is used in growth. Living things become larger and more complicated as they grow.

⊝ **SENSITIVITY** - Living things react to changes around them, such as touch, light, heat, cold, and sound.

⊝ **REPRODUCTION** - All living things produce young.

A HEALTHY, SPIRITUAL ECOSYSTEM

A healthy small-group ministry must be more like an organism than an organization because it's made up of individuals who are organic in nature. They *feed* on the revelation of Jesus Christ found in the Bible to obtain energy, grow, and stay healthy. With the help of the Holy Spirit, they exhibit internal *movement* by transforming from who they presently are into the people they truly are in Christ. Each individual *breathes* in the aroma of others' lives during good times and bad and exhales God's grace and peace. And every living being (including individuals and the small groups in which they gather) will ultimately *excrete* the baggage that creates darkness of the heart if it is going to remain healthy. Because they are *growing* and maturing, they are *sensitive* to the living things around them. When small-group members are living an organic lifestyle with one another, they cannot help but respond to the pain of others in the group and see the possibilities and the purposes of God alive in each other. Finally, when groups are organic, they *reproduce.* Group members tell others the story of Jesus and share their ongoing journeys of redemption so that those individuals can find the Jesus who is *"the way, the truth, and the life"* (John 14:6). When the group becomes too large to realistically allow its members to engage fully and effectively in one another's lives, they birth a new small group. This is the makeup of anything organic.

It is the responsibility of small-group leaders, coaches, and pastors to create and protect an environment in which the individual small-group member and every small group can live in a healthy, spiritual ecosystem. When this environment is produced and protected, the small-group garden will flourish and grow over time into a forest.

From the first page of this book to the very last, it's my goal to help you see, feel, know, apply, and embrace the techniques of a people gardener in creating and protecting the perfect environment for successful and organic small-group ministry.

EMBRACE THE ROLE OF A PEOPLE GARDENER

THE ROAD NOT TAKEN

Two roads diverged in a yellow wood,
And sorry I could not travel both
And be one traveler, long I stood
And looked down one as far as I could
To where it bent in the undergrowth;

Then took the other, as just as fair
And having perhaps the better claim,
Because it was grassy and wanted wear;
Though as for that, the passing there
Had worn them really about the same,

And both that morning equally lay
In leaves no step had trodden black
Oh, I kept the first for another day!
Yet knowing how way leads on to way,
I doubted if I should ever come back.

I shall be telling this with a sigh
Somewhere ages and ages hence:
two roads diverged in a wood, and I,
I took the one less traveled by,
And that has made all the difference. [2]

Robert Frost, 1920

DESTINATION:COMMUNITY

1 BASIC PRINCIPLES AND PRACTICES OF SMALL-GROUP LIFE

Our lives are full of decisions. At each fork in the road we must make choices. Each choice can impact our lives far more than we realize. The preceding poem by Robert Frost illustrates the emotional struggle we experience when forced to decide which path to take. Allow God to speak to your heart through this poem as you prepare to travel some unfamiliar paths.

Just as you can't plant a garden before tilling the ground, you can't begin a small-group ministry before learning the basic principles and practices of small-group life. Some of you will need to first remove the sod (other group leadership and training methodologies) before you till the ground. If you overlook this step, you'll force all the new vegetation you try to plant in your small-group ministry through the sod of past experience and an old, possibly ineffective knowledge or experience base.

Envision yourself as an Etch A Sketch® on which someone has created a picture of a small group. This picture represents your old group paradigm. In most instances, it will look like a Sunday School class you've attended in the past, a support group you've participated in, or perhaps an ineffective small group you've experienced. Now, turn yourself upside down and shake a bit. Then, turn yourself over. Clean slate, right? We need to remove any ineffective principles and/or practices that might have been instilled through other experiences and replace them with the small-group principles and practices that have proven effective for small-group ministry.

Each of the chapters in this section contains a principle or practice that is universal in small-group ministries. The first chapter will shift your paradigm from a "doing" group mentality to a "being" group lifestyle. Chapter 2 delves into the power of sharing our stories. In Chapter 3, you'll begin to embrace the adventure God has for you and your group. Chapter 4 gives you a vision of experiential discipleship. And finally, Chapter 5 will begin to ignite a vision for the outreach power of lives lived in community.

1 CHAPTER

AUTHENTICITY

"SOMETIMES I FEEL AS THOUGH I WERE BORN IN A CIRCUS, came out of my mother's womb like a man from a cannon, pitched toward the ceiling of the tent, all the doctors and nurses clapping in delight from the grandstand, the band going great guns in trombones and drums. I unfold and find flight hundreds of feet above the center ring, the smell of popcorn, the clowns gathered below amazed at my grace, all the people chanting my name as my arms come out like wings and move swan-like toward the apex where I draw them in, collapse my torso to my legs, roll over in perfection, then slowly give in to gravity, my body falling back toward the earth, the ground coming up so quick I can see the center ring growing beneath my weight.

And this is precisely when it occurs to me there is no net. And I wonder what is the use of a circus, and why a man should bother to be shot out of a cannon, and how fleeting is the applause of a crowd, and ... who is going to rescue me?" [3]

Donald Miller in Searching for God Knows What

DO YOU EVER FEEL LIKE YOU'VE BEEN SHOT OUT OF A CANNON?

You're performing well; you're hundreds of feet in the air; and you suddenly realize there is no net? Your world is a circus and you wonder, like Donald Miller, not who will rescue you, but whether or not anyone cares enough to even consider coming to your aid? Or maybe you've been unwilling to even admit that there is no net, unwilling to confess to yourself that life is confusing and/or chaotic.

Many Christ-followers have been deceived. We've been led to believe that the Christian life is a constant party—a series of celebrations planned and produced just for us as the guests of honor. In those weak moments when we try to place ourselves at the center of the universe, we might believe it's God's sole responsibility to make sure we're happy. It's absurd, but, if we're honest, we'll admit that we sometimes think this way. The truth is, the Christian life isn't always a party. God allows us to experience pain and discontentment so that we can, in time, reflect His glory. All of our ups and downs, masterpieces and mistakes, are designed to reshape us increasingly into the glorious image of God. The catch is that we were never designed to process these life experiences alone. We need to walk through life with others on the journey. We need community.

LIFE'S NOT A CONSTANT PARTY! PLENTY OF UPS AND DOWNS

Unfortunately, to our detriment, we often choose to live a solitary life, not because we want to be alone, but because we have not found a safe place in which we can unveil our true selves. We have trust issues, and we are quick to run from our problems instead of facing them. We run from authenticity when it is one of the keys to our spiritual growth. If we are ever going to reach life-altering levels of connectedness, our small groups must first acknowledge and embrace authenticity.

Authenticity is not consistency. Consistency can even mask or eradicate authenticity.

"Mr. Consistent Church Guy" came to group every week. He seemed like the model believer. He memorized Bible verses, read the latest Christian authors, took notes in church services, and volunteered to help the poor and needy. He was in high levels of church leadership and was very well respected. He went to work every day with a smile on his face and consistently told others about Jesus. His marriage was on track, and his kids were growing in Christ. He was consistently churchy, but down deep he was anything but happy, whole, and genuine. If he had been authentic, he would've admitted that he struggled with Internet pornography, that his anger got the best of him at times, and that he was verbally abusive to his family. Eventually, he divorced his wife and stopped attending church.

In order for a small group to be authentic, it must have seven key perspectives.

◉ THE MYSTERIES OF GOD FOUND IN THE BIBLE

Deuteronomy 29:29 reveals this fact: *"The secret things belong to the LORD our God, but the things revealed belong to us and to our children forever, that we may follow all the words of this law"* (NIV). Even God has secrets. As we've grown up surrounded by empiricism, vast amounts of information, and the cognitive focus of the modern age, we have been led down a theological path that requires us to come to final conclusions about everything we read in Scripture. Not everything God knows is revealed to us right now. Sometimes being authentic requires us to settle gracefully into the mystery of that which God understands but we will not be able to comprehend until we have a clear, perfect view of truth in heaven with Jesus. Authenticity while studying and discussing Scripture requires us to live in the mystery of God's powerful understanding and realize that there are ideas in the Scriptures that the human mind is not capable of comprehending. God is static, but our understanding of Him should be dynamic as He continues to reveal Himself to us.

SETTLE INTO MYSTERY
A DYNAMIC OF UNDERSTANDING GOD

◉ THE FACT THAT LIFE IS MESSY

Forrest Gump's mom was right. "Life is like a box of chocolates. You never know what you're gonna get." Life is a series of surprises, some good, some bad, and some downright debilitating. Solomon, the wisest man other than Jesus ever to walk on planet Earth, unsympathetically explains that there's *"a time to weep and a time to laugh, a time to mourn and a time to dance"* (Ecclesiastes 3:4). He blows out of the water the idea that the Christian life should lead us into a constant state of bliss. In other words, life is messy. When group members recognize that everyone's homes, jobs, minds, friendships, and marriages are messed up at some level, they begin to feel safe enough to share their own messes with others. And in sharing our messes, we become free to be ourselves and free to support one another as we continue the journey to be more like Jesus.

ALL OF US ARE MESSED UP

◉ PERSONAL IMPERFECTIONS

It's time for you to meet your author. I'm 5'9" (That may be a bit of an exaggeration … I *want* to be 5'9"). My gray goatee (I hate that word. It reminds me of an animal that will eat *anything!*) has one purpose: to cover up the double chin that resides elegantly (I think it's elegant) at the end of my round face. The rest of me is round, too. I tilt the scales at an enthusiastic 250 pounds! My hair grows straight up, and since I hate to spend time grooming, I gel it and go. The problem with my spike is my receding hairline, so I've occasionally been welcomed into a room with the title "Mo"—short for Mohawk. Dressing for success is not my thing. In fact, given the opportunity (although being married decreases the opportunities), I'll be stylin' in a pair of cutoff shorts and a Hawaiian shirt, both of which, I'm told, are no longer in style. And I recently found out that I have arthritis in both knees, which explains why I walk with a slight limp. According to many people, I am an imperfect physical being. But you know what? I just don't care what others think of me anymore.

I've learned to accept, even embrace, my imperfections, and I speak of them now with friends, some of whom are expected to hold me accountable for fixing what can be fixed. There was a time when the goal of my life was to reach perfection in all areas. I strove to have a Brad Pitt body, a Max Lucado writing style, and a Brad Johnson aptitude for leading and teaching (Brad has most recently been a pastor in California, and he's the greatest leader and preacher I've ever known). The pressure of these unrealistic goals crushed me. However, I achieved peace the day I realized that in order to be authentic, I had to accept myself the way I was. An honest acceptance of our imperfections is one of the keys to authenticity. We will judge ourselves, as well as those around us, until we accept our personal imperfections. Judgment and a critical spirit will keep a group from growing into true Christian community.

⊙ THAT GOD IS ALWAYS PRESENT EVEN WHEN HE FEELS DISTANT

God doesn't always seem close to us. There are times His silence during our struggles is intended to help us face our deep desire for connection and intimacy with Him or to persevere with hope through those dry times so that He can bring unexpected joys to us and others through them. God sometimes uses what we perceive as distance to force us to reach out to other believers. Let's not forget, believers are the Body of Christ, and Jesus is at work in our world through the spiritual gifts of this Body. Authentic people don't hide behind clichés and faith facades; instead, they talk about "the dark nights of the soul." In living honestly, they realize that God will use others in their group to remind them of His presence, power, and pursuit. Authentic group members remind each other that God may seem to be silent today, but He won't remain silent forever.

⊙ OTHERS AS INDIVIDUALS WITHOUT HAVING TO AGREE WITH ALL THEY DO AND SAY

God created us as individuals, and no two of us are exactly alike physically, philosophically, or spiritually. We're all on the spiritual journey, but none of us are at the exact same location. Differences shouldn't separate a small group. Instead, they should bring it together as group members benefit from one another's diverse perspectives and experiences. Emotionally healthy people are most apt to verbalize their disagreements with people they consider friends. Honesty that leads to disagreement may be a form of endearment.

⊙ CONFESSING OUR FAILURES AT THE RIGHT TIME WITH THE RIGHT PEOPLE

James, the first church elder and brother of Jesus, wrote, *"Confess your sins to each other and pray for each other so that you may be healed. The prayer of a righteous man is powerful and effective"* (James 5:16, NIV). Fear of exposure makes the mere thought of confession seem intimidating. Many people are afraid to become vulnerable. Deep down they fear that confessed information will be used against them as future ammunition.

Ultimately, they're afraid that people will pull away from them if the truth is discovered. The truth is, in most instances, when our moral failures are confessed to others in the right setting at the right time (with those who have covenanted to keep confidences and who care deeply about the confessor), the person confessing experiences healing. In a small group, the confession of sin will be most possible if members naturally, by their own accord, confess to those specific people in the group they have come to trust.

CONFESSION BRINGS HEALING

⊝ SATAN IS AT WORK IN OUR WORLD

To most people, Satan is a fictional character instead of *"the ruler of this world"* (John 12:31) until Jesus returns to establish His eternal kingdom. However, Christ-followers should know differently. They know Satan is an enemy who is on the attack, *"looking for anyone he can devour"* (1 Peter 5:8). He destroys friendships, family members, and belief systems. Most importantly, he kills hearts.

REAWAKEN YOUR HEART

In his book *Waking the Dead*, John Eldredge describes a part from *The Wonderful Wizard of Oz* that never made it into the movie. In the novel, the Tin Man is a real man who falls in love with a beautiful maiden whom he longs to marry. However, he won't marry her until he has enough money to build her a cottage. The Wicked Witch hates his love for the maiden, so she casts a spell on him that causes his limbs to be replaced with artificial ones made of tin. When Dorothy and the Scarecrow meet the Tin Man, he is ineffective and inefficient. His limbs are rusted, and he is unable to move. His axe is frozen in mid-air, and he can't speak. As they put oil on the joints around his mouth, he is able to speak and says:

"I little knew how cruel my enemy could be. She thought of a new way to kill my love for the beautiful Munchkin maiden, and made my axe slip again, so that it cut right through my body, splitting it into two halves. Once more the tinker came to my help and made me a body of tin ... But alas! I now had no heart, so that I lost my love for the Munchkin girl, and did not care whether I married her or not ... It was a terrible thing to undergo, but during the year I stood there I had time to think that the greatest loss I had known was the loss of my heart." [4]

Just like the Wicked Witch in the story, our enemy is after our hearts. If Satan can capture or kill our hearts, he robs us of the joy that comes from a heart fully alive. An authentic group admits it has an enemy and courageously engages in battle as a unified fighting force.

WHAT IS AUTHENTICITY IN SMALL GROUPS?

In simple terms, it's the willingness to openly share our pasts as well as what is continually unfolding in our present spiritual journeys. Small-group members will know they are living lives of authenticity when they are ready for their personal stories to be revealed ... the good and the bad, the successes, struggles and embarrassments.

NOTES

2 CHAPTER

LIFE IS A STORY

IN *WAKING THE DEAD*, author John Eldredge wrote, "Our life is a story. A rather long and complicated story that has unfolded over time. There are many scenes, large and small, and many 'firsts.' Your first step; your first word; your first day at school. There was your first best friend; your first recital; your first date; your first love; your first kiss; your first heartbreak. If you stop and think of it, your heart has lived through quite a story thus far. And over the course of that story your heart has learned many things. Some of what you learned is true; much of it is not." [5]

Because of our painful pasts, many of us see the future as a non-negotiable series of yet-to-be devastating experiences. We ask ourselves, "Where is the joy that God talks so much about in the Bible? Where is the peace of mind we are guaranteed? Why did God make promises He wasn't willing to keep?" The truth is that God does keep His promises, but we have a responsibility to journey into our own stories if we really want to experience the peace and joy that comes with being a child of God. The process begins with each of us remembering, realizing, verbalizing, processing, and diving into our past.

IN TO BE TOLD, Author Dan Allender points out in that we must answer some important questions before we enter into our stories. Our answers will help us to realize that God (the Author of our stories) cares deeply about us and longs for us to have "happily ever after" lives. They will also reveal how our past experiences are affecting our present lives. [6]

"WHAT SORT OF AUTHOR DO I HAVE?"

Allender says, "You are a story. You are not merely the possessor and teller of a number of stories; you are a well-written, intentional story that is authored by the greatest Writer of all time, and even before time and after time." God is the Author of our stories, and our Author is ultimately good, working all things together for our good (Romans 8:28).

"WHAT KINDS OF CHARACTERS POPULATE MY STORY?"

The people in our lives shape our stories. The major players are most likely Mom and Dad. Other influential characters include friends, brothers and sisters, grandparents, and surrogate parents. They can deeply affect our stories in both good and bad ways.

"WHAT SORT OF PLOT DOES MY STORY HAVE?"

Every story has a beginning, middle, and end. In fact, the plot of most stories includes 1) the background or situation, 2) the complication or conflict in the story, 3) the unveiling of flashbacks, tone, mood, and even irony during the story, 4) the turning point when conflict and suspense resolve, and 5) the return to normalcy for the protagonist.

If you look over your shoulder at your past and then forward into your present, you'll see that your past creates complications and conflicts for you today. When you become furious over the most minute problem, find yourself needing to be perfect, or expect your four-year-old to act like a full-grown adult, something from your past is producing those emotions and expectations. The Author of your story, longs for you to see the conflict subside and life return to the normalcy He originally designed. Life will return to paradise in eternity. For now, we journey together closer and closer to God, anticipating the glorious future.

"WHAT SORT OF ENDING AM I CO-WRITING?"

The ending of any story is the payoff for getting involved in the first place. While we can't choose whether or not we want to be in the story, God encourages us to affect the ending. While God is the primary Author, He welcomes us into the role of co-author. Our thoughts, words, and choices affect positively or negatively the direction of our stories.

Why do all of our stories include conflict, disappointment, and disillusionment? Because, all great stories have an antagonist, a villain. Your story—your life—is constantly under fire by your enemy, Satan. His ultimate goal is to keep you from enjoying a heart fully alive and a relationship with God that is intimate and authentic. We must heed the words of Solomon when he says, *"Above all else, guard your heart, for it is the wellspring of life"* (Proverbs 4:23, NIV).

ENGAGE IN CO-AUTHORING YOUR STORY

SATAN HAS A DIABOLICAL STRATEGY

The Enemy focuses on our life experiences. He lies to us about them and thereby distorts our view of ourselves, others, and God. He uses his warped version of our experiences to attack our hearts. Author and publisher Ron Keck explains, "Once we begin to recognize the battle being waged for our hearts and souls, the pain and struggles in our lives come into focus. The enemy strategically works to distort our identity—our perception of who we are. This distortion holds us back from the original glory we were created to enjoy and from deep intimacy with God. God has already sealed Satan's fate through Jesus' death and resurrection, but Satan is still 'prowling around' (1 Peter 5:8). He uses his primary tactic of deception to make us believe that God is not good, to put his twisted perspective on every event, to wreak pain and havoc in our lives, and, ultimately, to destroy us."

The following diagram from Ron Keck will help you understand the Enemy's battle plan. It describes the process of our hearts being captured and enslaved.

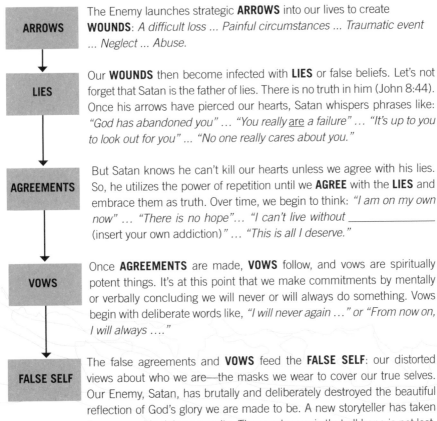

ARROWS

The Enemy launches strategic **ARROWS** into our lives to create **WOUNDS**: *A difficult loss ... Painful circumstances ... Traumatic event ... Neglect ... Abuse.*

LIES

Our **WOUNDS** then become infected with **LIES** or false beliefs. Let's not forget that Satan is the father of lies. There is no truth in him (John 8:44). Once his arrows have pierced our hearts, Satan whispers phrases like: *"God has abandoned you" ... "You really are a failure" ... "It's up to you to look out for you" ... "No one really cares about you."*

AGREEMENTS

But Satan knows he can't kill our hearts unless we agree with his lies. So, he utilizes the power of repetition until we **AGREE** with the **LIES** and embrace them as truth. Over time, we begin to think: *"I am on my own now" ... "There is no hope"... "I can't live without _____ (insert your own addiction)" ... "This is all I deserve."*

VOWS

Once **AGREEMENTS** are made, **VOWS** follow, and vows are spiritually potent things. It's at this point that we make commitments by mentally or verbally concluding we will never or will always do something. Vows begin with deliberate words like, *"I will never again ..."* or *"From now on, I will always ...."*

FALSE SELF

The false agreements and **VOWS** feed the **FALSE SELF**: our distorted views about who we are—the masks we wear to cover our true selves. Our Enemy, Satan, has brutally and deliberately destroyed the beautiful reflection of God's glory we are made to be. A new storyteller has taken the pen and is doing a rewrite. The good news is that all hope is not lost. **We can fight back!**

For though we live in the world, we do not wage war as the world does. The weapons we fight with are not the weapons of the world. On the contrary, they have divine power to demolish strongholds. We demolish arguments and every pretension that sets itself up against the knowledge of God, and we take captive every thought to make it obedient to Christ.

2 Corinthians 10:3-5, NIV

The way God designed our bodies is a model for understanding our lives together as a church: every part dependent on every other part, the parts we mention and the parts we don't, the parts we see and the parts we don't. If one part hurts, every other part is involved in the hurt, and in the healing. If on part flourishes, ever other part enters into the exuberance.

1 Corinthians 12:25-26, The Message

DEMOLISH STRONGHOLDS FIND THE HEALING POWER OF COMMUNITY

As God's people, we have access to divinely powerful weapons! Notice how many times the word "we" appears in 2 Corinthians 10:3-5. Developing community within a small group is one of the weapons we can use in our counterattack. We are more effective in the battle if we fight alongside others who are passionately pursuing the intermingling of their stories with the story of Jesus Christ. One of the ways we will defeat the Enemy is by being in a small group where Jesus is the centerpiece, the Holy Spirit is the Teacher, and God is given His rightful place as the Author of our stories. Victory will occur when group members fight diligently to release their own hearts first and then the hearts of their group members. Satan has emaciated all of us, but God longs to emancipate us. Healing occurs best in the context of community. *Our stories can be redeemed!*

EMBRACE REDEMPTION

3 CHAPTER

EMBRACE ADVENTURE DO LIFE TOGETHER

"ONCE UPON A TIME IN A LAND FAR, FAR AWAY ...."
"And they lived happily ever after." Each phrase indicates something very different is about to occur. "Once upon a time" announces that there is an adventure about to be revealed. Characters, including the hero and/or heroine and the antagonist, are about to be introduced. The storyline will be revealed, and the hero and/or heroine will do battle with the antagonist. "And they lived happily ever after" is a sigh of relief, an expression of unity. It sums up the fact that the antagonist is defeated, the conflict is at last resolved, and life is happy as it should be. But, have you ever really noticed that there is a battle raging between the "Once upon a time ..." and the "happily ever after"? Is the battle really over when we close the book? Often we mistakenly believe that the story has ended with the final period, as if the hero or heroine never experienced another quest. But life just isn't like that.

HAPPILY EVER AFTER

Do we really think that Simba from *The Lion King* never had to exercise his authority again to protect his royal throne or that the Beast from *Beauty and the Beast* never had another situation that made him act beastly? Isn't it naïve to assume that Cinderella and her Prince never had a problem teenager, or that Sleeping Beauty was awakened by the kiss of her adoring husband every morning of her peaceful existence?

Life is a series of disappointments and celebrations. Solomon described life well in Ecclesiastes 3:1-8. Read the following lines slowly. As you read, ask yourself this question: Would I rather live these experiences alone or with a group of people who support me and with whom I can celebrate?

DOING LIFE TOGETHER NOT JUST PLAYING CHURCH

> There is a time for everything, and a season for every activity under heaven:
> A time to be born and a time to die, a time to plant and a time to uproot,
> A time to kill and a time to heal, a time to tear down and a time to build,
> A time to weep and a time to laugh, a time to mourn and a time to dance,
> A time to scatter stones and a time to gather them,
> A time to embrace and a time to refrain,
> A time to search and a time to give up, a time to keep and a time to throw away,
> A time to tear and a time to mend, a time to be silent and a time to speak,
> A time to love and a time to hate, a time for war and a time for peace.
>
> **Ecclesiastes 3:1-8, NIV**

Small groups welcome the fact that life is a series of adventures and battles to be faced together. When a group of people does life together and doesn't just play at church, those in the group travel the winding, gypsy road as a band of brothers and sisters, fully engaged in life and passionate about those on the road with them. They cry on one another's shoulders, laugh together, enjoy the dance, work side-by-side, and go to battle for one another. While life is about the destination, it's even more about the people on the journey.

Take yourself back to the first time you heard the story of *The Lion King*, *Beauty and the Beast*, or *Cinderella*. Do you remember the warmth your heart felt at the "happily ever after" moment—the instant the two lovers walked off into the sunset? You didn't honestly believe they would never experience pain in life again. The warmth you felt was your heart resonating with peace because the hero and/or heroine in the story had found someone with whom they could share life. That's what "happily ever after" means. It means walking the journey of life together with others who care deeply.

One of the greatest adventures my wife and I have experienced together was raising our youngest son. He is one of the most creative, talented, intelligent, and loving people I know. However, for a while he chose to walk down destructive paths. I had counseled parents with adult children who were dancing with the Devil, and I had witnessed their pain, but I never thought I would experience that level of personal anguish. I was wrong. Over a three-year period, I felt so many emotions and believed so many lies: fear, anger, grief, despondency, hopelessness, rejection, blame, condemnation, denial, disillusionment with God, and disappointment in myself as a father. Eventually I was diagnosed with depression. It was a dark place and time. I now realize my son didn't cause any of these emotions. They were by-products of living on planet Earth.

I don't know if I would've survived during this time if it hadn't been for a small group of people of which I was a part. On multiple occasions during our meetings, I would share our story. Sometimes tears flowed and hugs were given. Often, similar stories of struggles with their own family members were shared. On one occasion, the group spent most of the meeting time just praying for my son. After that prayer time, I knew my wife and I weren't carrying our burden alone.

IT'S ESPECIALLY ABOUT THE PEOPLE ON THE JOURNEY

In Acts 2:44, Luke describes the first small groups by saying, *"Now all the believers were together and had everything in common."* To be honest, I'd read this verse a hundred times and it never really carried any meaning for me. That is, until the adventure that led me into a dark cave became too dangerous to continue alone. It was transforming to finally grasp how much we all share. Christ-followers share many similarities in this earthly life. We all share so much more than we ever realize or discuss, including:

- **FRUSTRATIONS**
- **CONFUSIONS**
- **MARRIAGE MISHAPS**
- **WORK STRUGGLES**
- **PAST BAGGAGE**
- **DISAPPOINTMENTS**
- **MISUNDERSTANDINGS**

- **INNER TURMOIL**
- **MYSTERIES TO EMBRACE**
- **OCCURRENCES TO LAUGH ABOUT**
- **MIRACLES FOR WHICH TO THANK GOD**
- **DREAMS TO REALIZE**
- **EXPERIENCES TO CELEBRATE**

A few years ago I opened one of the hundreds of e-mail forwards that were in my in-box, and I found a treasure. I don't know that it's accurate. I do know it's a captivating example of how small-group members share life together.

In 1976 at the Special Olympics track and field event in Spokane, Washington, nine contestants, all physically or mentally disabled, assembled at the starting line for the 100-yard dash. At the gun, they all started out, not exactly in a dash, but with a relish to run the race to the finish and win. All, that is, except one little boy who stumbled on the asphalt, tumbled over a couple of times, and began to cry. The other eight heard the boy cry. They slowed down and looked back. Then they all turned around and went back—every one of them.

One girl with Down syndrome bent down and kissed him and said, "This will make it better." Then all nine linked arms and crossed the finish line together. Everyone in the stadium stood, and the cheering went on for several minutes.

What a touching picture of community! It is a powerful expression of something about which I am passionate—people being discipled or spiritually developed and matured within a redemptive community. I like the phrase "experiential discipleship." Turn the page, and you'll get a glimpse of how this works.

4

CHAPTER

EXPERIENTIAL DISCIPLESHIP

ONE OF THE LAST DIRECTIVES JESUS GAVE TO HIS DISCIPLES was for them to "make disciples" (Matthew 28:19). He wanted them to do for others what He had done for them. Jesus discipled experientially. As Jesus and His 12 apostles ate, rested, and traveled together, Jesus often paused to teach them. He used visual object lessons to establish necessary principles, and He challenged them to carry out tasks that were far beyond their comfort zones. He helped them to evaluate their hearts so they could realize the motives behind their actions, and He used everyday life experiences to help them process the truth. Most importantly, He modeled what they were to do once He left them. Jesus' experiential teaching style created a safe learning environment in which His disciples could grow and mature. Jesus wanted them in turn to continue the process of living in community with others and making them disciples.

KNOWLEDGE IS NOT ENOUGH

Making disciples is about far more than imparting information and knowledge. There are certain things small-group members must experience, not simply know about, before they can become mature disciples. The goals of every small-group ministry and every small-group leader should focus on creating an environment that fosters the following six key experiential components:

◉ EXPERIENCE 1 — A Small-Group Leader with High Expectations
An effective small-group leader challenges group members to move out of their comfort zones in order to grow. One of the keys to spiritual growth is to know and then live out God's clear directions from the Bible (James 1:22). God sets the bar high for our attitudes, beliefs, and behaviors. He does this not because He's a demanding, tyrannical taskmaster, but because He ultimately knows what will make life good for us and for others around us. God is passionate about His people and longs for us to live life in abundance—to experience all that He has for us!

Within the safety and support of a small group, as group members become aware of attitudes that are out of line, behaviors that are unhealthy or destructive in the long run, or paradigms that need to be overhauled, the leader can gently move group members toward understanding, inside out transformation, and action.

OUT OF THEIR COMFORT ZONES

Spiritual growth will tend to follow these phases:

Phase 1: A group member recognizes an unmet biblical expectation.

Phase 2: The individual experiences discomfort as he becomes aware of the need for change.

Phase 3: The small-group leader wisely guides the group member toward change from the inside out, recognizing that what we believe in our innermost being (Psalm 51:6) drives our behavior.

Phase 4: The small-group member decides to do what's right and good rather than what's easy.

Phase 5: The small-group member engages the process of transformation.

Phase 6: The leader and small-group members celebrate with the individual who has courageously moved beyond his comfort zone.

Phase 7: The individual experiences growth and is more easily motivated to take on the next challenge into which God may call him.

◉ EXPERIENCE 2 — Spiritual Gifts at Work in the Small Group
As each person invites Jesus into his or her life as personal Savior and is adopted into God's family, he or she is supernaturally given a spiritual gift by the Holy Spirit.

These gifts are God's way of making sure no need goes unmet and everyone is effectively serving others within the circle of influence. When individuals actively exercise their spiritual gifts within the context of a small group, growth takes place. When members use their spiritual gifts to meet the needs of other people in the group, they realize God's power is real and flowing through them. As they cautiously step out in faith to discover, explore, and activate their spiritual gifts, group members experience courageous Christianity.

REAL POWER FLOWING THROUGH US

➲ EXPERIENCE 3 – Processing Life's Struggles Through the Eyes of Faith

James writes, *"Consider it a great joy, my brothers, whenever you experience various trials, knowing that the testing of your faith produces endurance. But endurance must do its complete work, so that you may be mature and complete, lacking nothing"* (James 1:2-4). Our trials offer us one of the greatest opportunities for spiritual growth if they are processed with other Christ-followers through the eyes of faith and truth. Following are key steps small-group leaders should keep in mind as they support other group members as they face struggles on their journeys toward spiritual growth:

Step 1 – **Stop and Remember.** Remembering and grieving our losses is vital to healing and growth. Jesus promised, *"Blessed are those who mourn, because they will be comforted"* (Matthew 5:4).

Step 2 – **Be Self-Aware.** We need to ask ourselves why we reacted as we did, why we feel as we do, why a certain event brought these emotions to the surface. A small group can act as the mirror that you need to see yourself accurately.

Step 3 – **Stay in Your Pain.** In Hebrews 12:2, Jesus models a critical formula for healing that we often get backwards: *"who for the joy that lay before Him <u>endured a cross</u> and <u>despised the shame</u>, and has sat down at the right hand of God's throne"* (emphasis added). Jesus endured or embraced His pain and rejected His shame.

EMBRACE OUR PAIN, REJECT OUR SHAME

Step 4 – **Open up to Others.** Especially in the midst of struggles, it's vital to get others involved in the process. God never intended us to fight through life alone; He designed us to live in an interdependent community. The Villain in our stories would love to isolate us, aggressively target our weaknesses, and take us out. We need someone to do battle alongside us (James 5:16). Healing occurs best in the context of community—when others join us on the journey. We also need the encouragement and accountability of others who care about us (Ecclesiastes 4:9-12).

Step 5 – **Develop a Desire To Change.** Once we open up and share our struggles, we must also take the next step by expressing a heartfelt willingness to repent—to change the course of our lives. Grief over the pain and losses of life leads to a willingness to confess our failures before God and close friends. Our journey begins when we honestly admit the condition of our lives rather than denying the truth or blaming others.

Step 6 – **Be Transformed.** Unfortunately, the word *repent* has gained a bad connotation over the years. Most people immediately think about hellfire preaching and condemnation. Actually, "repent" comes from the Greek word *metanoia*, which means to change (*meta*) our mind-set or understanding (*noia*). The word *metamorphosis* is a related term, meaning a change in form or substance, and is used to describe what occurs when a caterpillar retreats into its cocoon to emerge as a butterfly. As we recognize the battle being waged over our minds and hearts, it becomes clearer why change must occur from the inside out, beginning in our innermost being—our hearts and minds (Psalm 51:6; Romans 12:1-2). Our actions follow our truest and deepest beliefs.

Step 7 – **See Through the Eyes of Faith**. More than anything else, the healing journey requires us to trust God. Healing the wounds in our innermost being will lead us down paths we never could have imagined. Together, we must take one day and one step at a time as we walk into the shadows with Jesus, allow Him to turn the shadows to light, ease our pain, and lead us into freedom, truth, and the true desires of our hearts. In Isaiah 42:16, God explains why trust is vital: *"I will lead the blind by ways they have not known, along unfamiliar paths I will guide them; I will turn the darkness into light before them and make the rough places smooth. These are the things I will do; I will not forsake them"* (NIV). Faith always leads to action. *"In the same way, faith by itself, if it is not accompanied by action, is dead "* (James 2:17, NIV).

☉ EXPERIENCE 4 – Experiential Meetings and Gatherings
Small groups are made up of people who connect throughout the week as they share life together. However, the small-group meeting offers a leader the greatest opportunity to experientially pass on life lessons to the entire group. During meeting times, members can connect personally to an experience that reveals certain truths in the Bible. These moments offer a leader the perfect opportunity to create personal moments that lead to heart transformation.

☉ EXPERIENCE 5 – Seeing God at Work
God makes over 7,000 promises to us in the Bible. When someone in the group sees one of these promises fulfilled, or when a prayer is answered, the group needs to celebrate. When a group leader recognizes God working through either a positive or a difficult time and guides the group to celebrate together, the group's level of faith grows exponentially.

Some creative ways to experientially celebrate when God works:

1. Decorate your meeting room and throw a party. Play party music as the recipient of God's redemptive work enters the room. Serve a cake that says, "Congratulations," "Journey On," or "God Rocks." Read the fulfilled promise from Scripture and thank God for caring enough to respond to the group's prayers.

2. Bury the situation. Have a funeral and bury the problem in the back yard. Simply write down a word or two that depicts the situation on something that is biodegradable. During a group meeting, dig a small hole in the yard and bury the problem in it. Ceremonially place the situation in the hole and explain that God has dealt with it. The beauty of this experience is that if the person chooses to embrace the buried attitude or paradigm again, you can go back and dig it up to remind them that it is no more.

3. Burn the situation. Ask the person whose prayer has been answered to write a brief history of the problem and, if they'd like, a description of the feelings they've suffered because of it. Go somewhere with the group where there's a place to build a campfire (doing this in the backyard grill or fireplace would be effective enough). Have everyone stand around the campfire. Ask the person to share what he or she has written on the piece of paper. Then, read 2 Samuel 22:7-20 and instruct the person to throw the sheet of paper that describes the situation into the fire. Remind the person that it is no more. Highlight that God wants to come to our rescue because He delights in us. Let the other group members pray and thank God for setting the person free.

⊜ EXPERIENCE 6 – Growth that Flows from Spiritual Passion Promoters

We can all recite a list of what's typically referred to as "spiritual disciplines," most of which tend to be drudgery. Even the word "disciplines" connotes things that we make ourselves do because they're unpleasant, but somehow good for us. How is it that conversing with our Friend, Father, and Bridegroom, knowing His story and His heart, capturing truths that lead to an amazing life, passionately expressing in worship our love for the One who first loved us, turning to our Rescuer in times of need for ourselves and others, and telling others the story of Jesus the Hero who came to set us free has deteriorated into the *forced disciplines* of prayer, Bible reading and memorization, journaling, worship, petition, and evangelism?

WE MUST REKINDLE THE FIRES

My wife and I dated a little less than a year before we married. When I met her, I knew that she was the one. I did everything I could to know her better. If there had been a book about Julie Clay, I'd have read it. If there had been a class about her history, I'd have been the first one to register. If there had been a way to listen in on her conversations (by the way, I did sometimes sit at a table close enough to hers in the cafeteria so that I could simply hear her voice), I'd have done that. Why? I wasn't motivated by a need to check off a list of everything that had to be done to win her love. I chose to spend time in these "passion promoters" so that I could know her better and build an even deeper love for her.

WARNING! Many Christ-followers have been on the road to a truly intimate relationship with Jesus only to be suddenly blind-sided by someone informing them that the spiritual life is all about following a set of disciplines. Before they know it, all the life and passion in their relationship has been lost, and they feel separated from their Lover, Jesus. Now, I'm not suggesting that the spiritual disciplines are unnecessary for spiritual growth. On the contrary! I believe they are vital to spiritual growth. But let's stop calling them and treating them as disciplines. Let's call them "passion promoters" because approached with the right attitude, they promote a passionate relationship with Jesus. The purpose of these disciplines is to grow within us a deep love relationship with Jesus.

[Jesus speaking:] "To the angel of the church in Ephesus write: These are the words of him who holds the seven stars in his right hand and walks among the seven golden lampstands: I know your deeds, your hard work and your perseverance. I know that you cannot tolerate wicked men, that you have tested those who claim to be apostles but are not, and have found them false. You have persevered and have endured hardships for my name, and have not grown weary. Yet I hold this against you: You have forsaken your first love."

Revelation 2:1-4, NIV

As you can see, experiential discipleship done in a small-group setting is a synergistic experience. Each person in the group realizes an equal responsibility to move the rest of the group toward maturity. The leader of the group must take on the commitment of creating an environment where people understand their responsibilities to one another and are encouraged and given the freedom to act on behalf of the other members of the group.

LEADERS CREATE THE ENVIRONMENT FOR GROWTH

5 CHAPTER

COMPELLING COMMUNITY

THERE'S SOMETHING ATTRACTIVE TO ALL OF US ABOUT THE THEME SONG FROM THE HIT TV SERIES CHEERS:

Making your way in the world today takes everything you've got. Taking a break from all your worries sure would help a lot. Wouldn't you like to get away?
All those nights when you've got no lights, the check is in the mail.
And your little angel hung the cat up by its tail.
And your third fiancé didn't show!
Sometimes you wanna go …
Where everybody knows your name, and they're always glad you came.
You wanna be where you can see the troubles are all the same.
You wanna be where everybody knows your name
You roll out of bed, Mr. Coffee® is dead, the morning's looking bright
And your shrink ran off to Europe, and didn't even write.
And your husband wants to be a girl!
Be glad there's one place in the world
Where everybody knows your name, and they're always glad you came.
You wanna go where people know, people are all the same.
You wanna go where everybody knows your name.
Where everybody knows your name. And they're always glad you came. [7]

ALWAYS GLAD YOU CAME

The song "Where Everybody Knows Your Name" touches a chord within each one of us, acknowledging that life is messy and flat out difficult at times. If only there were a place where we could enjoy a shelter from the storms of life—"where ... they're always glad [we] came." This song speaks to our deep desires for community, support, transparency, authenticity, and acceptance. If only such a place existed, people would line up at the doors to join. It's too bad that this song was written about a bar rather than a church.

DEEP DESIRES FOR COMMUNITY, AUTHENTICITY, AND ACCEPTANCE

I received an e-mail a few years ago that described the following story. As the story goes, a junior high school hired a new teacher who was an atheist and proud of it. He was always talking about his beliefs (or lack thereof), and since the kids were fairly young, he intimidated them. One day he announced, "My mother was atheist, my father was an atheist, and I'm an atheist. How many in this room are atheists?" The kids were a little scared of him. They all raised their hands except for one little girl. He asked her, "Well, what are you, then?" She said, "I'm a Christian. My mother is a Christian, my father is a Christian, and I'm a Christian, too." He responded, "If your mother was a moron, and your father was a moron, what would that make you?" She replied, "I guess that would probably make me an atheist."

Many people have laughed hysterically at this story. I'm one of them. I rolled on the floor and belly laughed. That is, until 60 seconds into my hilarious outburst when I heard the Holy Spirit question my attitude about people who need Jesus. In that moment, I realized that I lacked a love for people who are the farthest from Jesus. I wondered how I could reach people who are far from Christ, but I knew the answer. Compelling Community.

SIMPLY IRRESISTIBLE

A group unwilling to settle for anything less than redemptive community will be compelling—irresistible to people in search of acceptance and significance. Compelling Community embodies the elements of "Everybody Knows Your Name" and more. Real community like this will be a magnet for our searching, unbelieving world. Even now, pre-Christians are going about their daily routines when a group of authentic believers welcomes them into their inner circle. These people discover a whole new way of living that is captivating, exhilarating, and life giving. Even though they might be skeptical about all the Jesus and church talk, they are drawn to the unity of purpose, the warmth of people who care for one another, the spirit of oneness, and the power that comes from the personality bigger than the group itself—the personality of Jesus living in and through a thriving small group.

When pre-Christians see believers living authentic, Spirit-led, connected lives, their initial fascination becomes curiosity. Curiosity evolves into understanding, and understanding leads to spiritual awareness. Spiritual awareness points to a personal encounter with Jesus and a resulting life transformation. This is why Jesus says, *"I give you a new commandment: love one another. Just as I have loved you, you must also love one another. By this all people will know that you are My disciples, if you have love for one another"* (John 13:34-35). Proving our love for one another is the most effective way to help others see the Jesus we know. Living life together as Jesus envisioned in the presence of a pre-Christian is Compelling Community and a powerful form of team evangelism.

WHAT DRIVES CHRISTIANS IS DIFFERENT AND MORE SUBSTANTIVE

Evangelism through Compelling Community simply invites unbelievers to share life with a group of authentic Christ-followers in an authentic, redemptive small group. It's simply asking a non-believer to become an equal in the small group you're leading. As pre-Christians watch group members exercise their love for one another through sacrificial giving, meeting one another's needs, caring for one another, and spurring one another on to growth, they can't help but realize that what drives Christians is different and more substantive than the world they experience at work, the local pub, and even in their own home. And as they see believers worshipping their God together passionately and hear them speak of Him meeting their needs and helping them through life's dark situations, they begin to believe He will do the same for them.

MANY PEOPLE ARE WIRED, BUT FEW ARE REALLY CONNECTED

POTENT EVANGELISM

Evangelism through Compelling Community is most potent in today's postmodern world—a world full of people unapologetically hesitant to believe the Bible is truth. People today are cynical about what they hear in a preacher's monologue, but they will welcome a dialogue on a spiritual or real-life topic. They are willing to journey into their pasts because they understand that it affects their presents and futures. They long for a few close relationships rather than a myriad of passive acquaintances. With all the technological advances of recent years, there seem to be more and more ways to get connected with other people. Unfortunately, many people are wired, but few are really connected. Small groups are the perfect environments in which this postmodern generation can really connect with other people and meet Jesus. Pre-Christians today are powerfully affected when they see people of faith in a healthy small group, as they give and receive genuine love while sharing life together in an unpretentious and authentic way.

COMPELLING COMMUNITY IS POTENT IN A POSTMODERN WORLD

SECTION TWO
THE HEART OF LEADERSHIP

"**EVERYTHING RISES AND FALLS** *on leadership.*"
- John Maxwell

"For lack of guidance a nation falls, but many advisers make victory sure."   - Proverbs 11:14, NIV

"Some men see the world as it is and ask why; others see the world as it might be and ask why not."   - Bernard Shaw

"The task of the leader is to get his people from where they are to where they have not been."   - Henry Kissinger

"A leader is a dealer in hope."   - Napoleon Bonaparte

If you think you're leading, just look behind you. If no one is following, you're just out taking a walk.   - Unknown

"Lead, follow, or get out of the way."   - Thomas Paine

"Leaders take the personal time and effort to get involved while others are sitting in easy chairs."   - John Ben Shepperd

"An ability to embrace new ideas, routinely challenge old ones, and live with paradox will be the effective leaders premier trait."   - Tom Peters

"Leaders do not know some things are impossible, they just proceed to get them done."   - John Ben Shepperd

2 SMALL-GROUP LEADERSHIP

People need and long to be led by someone they trust. A passionate leader with a concrete vision is possibly the most important factor in any small-group endeavor. If you look through the Bible, you'll find that God seldom sends a team. He sends out one leader to spearhead a project or direct a movement.

That leader becomes the catalyst for gathering, mentoring, and motivating a group of people so that a God-given vision becomes a reality. Small-group ministry is no different. Whether you're leading one small group, coaching five groups, or shepherding the entire small-group ministry, in order for your vision to become a reality, you must lead people effectively and diligently.

Leadership is the ability to obtain and retain followers and organize, unify, and direct them to accomplish a God-given vision. The five essential verbs are ...

1) OBTAIN

2) RETAIN

3) ORGANIZE

4) UNIFY

5) DIRECT

Over the next five chapters, it is my goal for you to begin to grasp these concepts as they relate to the people who will be in your small group(s).

6

OBTAINING GROUP MEMBERS

THE GROUP YOU'RE GOING TO LEAD IS MADE UP of people who believe small groups are primarily about relationships. If they join your small group and begin to feel as though the group's primary goal is to gain members, they will bail quickly. You will also lose members if the group's focus is on getting through a particular curriculum or planning fun get-togethers. Don't get me wrong. There are many kinds of small groups (prayer groups, Bible-study groups, ministry groups, and so on), but when you say "small group" most people think of a group that is relationship-driven. If, after attending a few weeks, your members believe they've been duped, they won't stick around.

Leaders must invite people into their lives, not their programs

HOW DO YOU RECRUIT YOUR SMALL GROUP?

1. PRAY

Jesus spent meaningful time praying before He recruited his apostles. You should do the same. Ask God to guide you to the people He wants you to invite into your group—people who are longing for a heart change and people who want to join you on the journey. You will need members who will be willing to share their stories over time with the group and involve themselves in everyone else's stories. Pray for people who will allow God's Spirit and the Bible to guide them about life's situations, and ask for people who will truly want to experience authentic redemptive community. Also, begin praying from the very beginning that God will lead you to people who are not yet followers of Jesus to become part of your small group.

ASK GOD TO GUIDE YOU TO PEOPLE WHO WANT TO JOIN YOU ON THE JOURNEY

2. CLEARLY COMMUNICATE THE GROUP'S FOCUS

There are many types of small groups. It's important that the people you invite to join your group are people who are anticipating the same outcomes as you. Bill Donohue identifies five primary types of small groups [8] and I have added one more:

1. Disciples-Making Groups – for Christ-followers who want to develop spiritually.

2. Community Groups – for Christ-followers and pre-Christians who want to build in-depth relationships with others.

3. Service Groups – for Christ-followers and pre-Christians who are serving alongside one another in ministry (ushers, musical teams, leadership teams, outreach teams, and the like).

4. Seeker Groups – predominantly for pre-Christians who are dealing with questions before trusting their lives to Jesus.

5. Support Groups – for Christ-followers and pre-Christians who are seeking support through personal difficulties.

6. Healing Groups – for Christ-followers and pre-Christians who need to be released from the lies and bondage that trap their hearts and can potentially ruin their lives.

WHAT'S THE FOCUS OF MY GROUP?

When you ask people to join a small group, they have preconceived notions concerning what that group will be doing and how the group will function. They may be thinking they're getting involved in a service group when the group will be a support group. Or they may think they're joining a healing group only to find out after a few weeks they're in a community group. The people you invite into your group should want to be involved in the same activities, experiences, and outcomes that your group is going to be about. There are few things more devastating to a new small group than the quick exit of people because of a lack of communication concerning the group's focus.

MAKE PEOPLE AWARE OF THE GROUP'S PRIMARY AGENDA

When you're recruiting people into your small group, you want to be certain they are very aware of the group's primary agenda. For instance, if you're leading a disciple-making group, you'll want to say to the individual you're inviting, "This group is for Christ-followers who want to develop spiritual depth." If you're asking someone to join you in a community group, be certain you tell them the group is for Christ-followers and pre-Christians who want to build in-depth relationships with a group of people. Once the person you're speaking with becomes excited about what the group will be doing, invite them to join.

INVITE PEOPLE INTO YOUR LIFE, NOT YOUR PROGRAM
INVITE PEOPLE EXCITED ABOUT THE GROUP'S JOURNEY

3. CLARIFY THE RECRUIT'S LEVEL OF COMMITMENT

If possible, give the person considering your group some understanding of the amount of commitment and individual heart work that will be involved. The following questions are on the minds of most people who are considering whether or not to join a small group:

TOP TEN LIST: Ten Questions Potential Small-Group Members Ask

1. How much of my time is this going to take?
2. What are we going to do with our children during meetings?
3. Will there be homework? If so, how much?
4. Am I going to have to talk or can I just sit and listen during meetings?
5. Will I have to pray out loud?
6. Who else is going to be in the group?
7. How much do I have to know about the Bible?
8. How many weeks or months is this group going to last?
9. If I don't like it, can I leave without people being angry with me?
10. What are we going to be doing during meetings?

The answers to these questions will help to determine whether or not someone is willing to be a part of your group. For example, there is a high level of intimidation that surrounds a healing group. Attendees intuitively know that they will need to explore and share parts of themselves that have never before been visited or revealed. They will most likely be willing, but hesitant. They need to be told in the recruitment process that there will be heart homework involved and that they will need to involve themselves in every aspect of the group's life or the entire group will be negatively affected.

EXPLAIN EXPECTATIONS FOR HEART HOMEWORK

Larry and Nancy came from a very different church background than ours. They knew a key focus in our church was small community groups, but they had no idea what they were in for. Without a clear enough understanding of the group's purpose or the couple's commitment, Larry joined with great hesitancy and Nancy with great anticipation.

As the group members began to bond and feel closer and safer with one another, they started to open up in sharing struggles and personal stories. As Nancy began to come out and embrace the group, Larry continued to withdraw, interacting only on an intellectual level. Other group members became concerned for Larry, so a couple of us gently approached him. We had a good discussion and realized in the process that Larry was just not accustomed to, nor comfortable with, sharing his story.

In the end, Larry decided to leave the group, and the couple soon left the church to find a place where Larry could be comfortable. Fortunately, the couple and the group parted peacefully, but this is not always the case.

As you can see, gathering a group of people who are passionately pursuing the journey you're going to take them on demands more than posting a sign up sheet. If you strategically enlist the members for your group, you will have a much greater chance of accomplishing the group's goals. So, where do you look for potential group members? Focus on your entire community, not just your church population. The following ideas may help you connect with people who might be thinking about joining a small group. I've gathered these ideas from small-group leaders around the country.

STRATEGICALLY ENLIST MEMBERS FOR YOUR GROUP

RECRUITING IDEAS

1. MAIL: Prepare a letter that gives the following information: a) that you are starting a small group; b) what the group's goal will be; c) how long the group will meet; and d) why you're starting the group. Mail the letter to people you are inviting and then follow up with those individuals by telephone a few days after they receive the letter. At the first meeting, discuss "The Top Ten" list with the people gathered.

2. MEETING: Have an open meeting at your church. Use the worship guide, posters, and announcements from the pulpit to make people aware that a new small group is forming and announce an open meeting for anyone interested in becoming part of the group. Hold a meeting where you unveil answers to "The Top Ten" list.

3. PERSONAL INVITATION: The most effective way to welcome people into your group is by personal invitation. If you choose to recruit the people in your group by face-to-face conversation, be certain you make the invitation substantive. Make the people you invite aware of the answers to "The Top Ten" list. If your group will be a healing group or redemptive community group, stress that the group will be composed of people who are deeply involved in one another's lives.

PERSONAL INVITATIONS ARE MOST EFFECTIVE

4. PRESENTATION: Churches with the necessary resources can make people aware of small-group opportunities by utilizing dramatic presentations and video spots in worship. These presentations can be followed by an announcement that will most often highlight the date of a meeting for interested people. You could also place someone at a kiosk in the lobby to answer questions. Again, use "The Top Ten" list to prepare for potential questions.

5. MEDIA OUTLETS: If the goal of your group is to reach the community, running newspaper ads or securing free space on local radio or TV to announce the opportunity can be effective. Make sure interested people are made aware of a Web site and phone number for more information. The Web site, as well as the people taking phone calls, should explain when the first Q and A meeting will be (again "The Top Ten" list will answer most questions people will ask) and that sign up for the group will take place at the end of the meeting.

EVERYONE NEEDS WHAT SMALL GOUPS OFFER!

Remember this ... Everyone needs what small groups offer. As you go about recruiting individuals to join your group, open your heart and your mind to everyone. Don't allow personal biases or negative histories to keep you from inviting someone to join. Some of your most fulfilling times will be when you see someone who you thought would never last with a small group become powerfully transformed by the experience.

NOTES

7 CHAPTER

RETAINING GROUP MEMBERS

GETTING PEOPLE TO JOIN YOUR GROUP is exciting and downright exhilarating! But getting them and keeping them are two very different things. People often join a group only to quit after a few meetings. In order to retain your group members and accomplish your dreams for the group, you will have to purposefully do these two things:

1) Lead well
2) Involve the members of your group in meaningful ways

LEAD WELL

Small-group leadership is all about people. It's about longing to see your vision become a reality while you work alongside the people you are discipling. Ken Blanchard, Patricia Zigarmi, and Drea Zigmari remind us in *Leadership and the One Minute Manager®* that "Leadership is not something you do to people. It's something you do with people." [9] Great leaders work with people and realize that they are equals with different roles.

LOVE, PROTECT, NURTURE, AND STRETCH PEOPLE

A small-group leader loves, protects, nurtures, and stretches the people he or she is taking on a journey to maturity. Too many leaders use people to accomplish their vision without considering those people's needs. These driven leaders target only the bull's-eye of accomplishment. They completely overlook the importance of the hearts they recruited to work alongside them. A leader like this has tunnel vision, focusing only on his or her objective. Because of their tunnel vision, they don't see the people around them who are suffering because their leader has no concern for their needs or their future.

There are two basic types of leaders: the one who leads and develops people while carrying out an objective and the one who uses people to accomplish an objective. This diagram highlights key differences between these two types of leaders:

LEADS PEOPLE	USES PEOPLE TO ACCOMPLISH OBJECTIVES
- Cares about people	- Needs workers
- Recruits people	- Gathers laborers
- Trains and develops people	- Directs people
- Empowers people	- Drops people when the job is complete

Your most important concern must be the people in your group. Transforming their hearts is the objective. Having fantastic Bible studies and prayer times, getting new people to join your church, even becoming best friends cannot be the marker of your success. You will be successful if the people in your group are being transformed. A transformational small group forms because a leader cares deeply about the individuals in his or her group.

SUCCESS ... TRANSFORMED LIVES

When you engage people to work alongside you as a team, you'll retain group members. Working as a team involves your group members' minds, bodies, and hearts. They'll work passionately because you've given them ownership in the group. As their input is given, received, and utilized, they'll feel good about themselves and the team. If you show people respect, that respect breeds mutual admiration and unity.

As in raising children, love and commitment are foundational to the next step of training group members to carry out a personally fulfilling role in the group. Then, empower them to do the work you've prepared them to do. Gene Wilkes in his study *Jesus on Leadership* explains, "Team leaders are more like a soccer player than a golfer on tour. They are not lone rangers. They involve others to reach a shared goal. Team leaders are player coaches." [10] When you care mostly about the people and create a team that's working together toward the common goal of a transformational small group, you will retain your group members.

INVOLVE GROUP MEMBERS IN MEANINGFUL WAYS

Group members will be much more apt to continue with the group over the long haul if they feel a meaningful level of ownership and responsibility in the group. In order for group members to sense ownership, there are six things they deserve.

MEANINGFUL LEVELS OF OWNERSHIP HELP PEOPLE TO CONTINUE

1. **THEY DESERVE TO SEE THE VISION.** It's the responsibility of the small-group leader to express the vision in such a fashion that group members become desperate to see that vision become a reality. Vision focuses the group. (See Section 3, Chapter 12.)

2. **THEY DESERVE TO KNOW THE GOALS.** Goals energize a small group. Goals should be measurable. Some goals a group might adopt are to get three pre-Christians to become part of the group, to spend three weekends together on mission, never to miss a meeting unless there's a death in the family, to get together just for fun once a month, to pray daily for one another, to be available for one another, and to see the fruit of transformed lives.

3. **THEY DESERVE TO HELP PREPARE THE STRATEGY NECESSARY TO ACCOMPLISH THE GOALS.** If a small group sets goals without creating strategies to accomplish those goals, the goals will most likely never be met. Strategies are vital because they organize the group to accomplish the goals that have been determined. It's important to involve group members in developing strategies. The outcome will likely be much better than what you would create alone and will develop a healthy level of ownership. And when people have ownership, they willingly give their time and effort to executing the strategy.

4. **THEY DESERVE TO BE INVITED INTO THE ADVENTURE.** Small-group members who see the group's vision will help to set the goals and establish the strategies to accomplish those goals, and they are excited about doing their parts. As members are encouraged to exercise their natural abilities and spiritual gifts, they'll feel satisfaction because they want to be a part of something vital and significant. Growth naturally occurs when a person is encouraged to go beyond present abilities and comfort zones.

I learned how important it is to allow small-group members to participate in the ministry's work the hard way. While on staff at a church in Kentucky, a small group I was leading worked together on the first three phases just unveiled. Because I knew the busy schedules of the people in my group, I found myself taking on most of the workload. In one of our meetings, I was reporting on the work that had been completed that week when one of the members asked, "When do we get to be involved?" I was ambushed. My mentality was that people really didn't want to do the hard work. The truth was, they did. People who buy into the vision of the group and feel a deep sense of ownership can't wait to roll up their sleeves. Don't rob them of this opportunity for growth and fulfillment.

5. **THEY DESERVE TO EVALUATE PROGRESS.** All great small groups evaluate group life together. They evaluate if they're accomplishing the goals they set and if they're keeping the group covenant. They also evaluate each strategic experience after its completion. Evaluation enables the group to modify some aspect of a strategy or revisit shared goals. Evaluation is vital not only to the retention of group members but also to the level of ownership group members feel to the group. Each time your group spends time in evaluation, members are reminded of the group's vision, goals, and strategies. This re-energizes people.

CELEBRATION IS THE OFTEN OVERLOOKED GLUE OF GROUP LIFE

6. **THEY DESERVE TO CELEBRATE ACCOMPLISHMENT.** Celebration unifies a team forever. However, it is often the overlooked glue of group life. All too often we set goals, create strategies, work hard, and see amazing goals come to fruition only to begin working on the next experience or event. We skip the most important bonding experience— celebration. Celebrating together is fitting anytime God does something wonderful, such as enabling you to reach a milestone. Evaluate, then celebrate, no matter how negative the evaluation is. We need to celebrate the completion of a project as well as its effectiveness.

What you've just read may go against everything you've always believed to be true about small-group life. You may have believed that the less people had to give, the more likely they were to stick around. Not so! Most people tend to give as much time as necessary to something that's captured their hearts. And most people don't give their hearts to a cause until they've gotten their hands dirty first. Be a great leader and give your group members ownership, allowing them to be involved in the process of preparation and accomplishment at all levels. Guide, guard, nurture, and cherish them throughout your time together, and most of your people will be fully committed to you and your group.

PEOPLE STAY AND WORK IF YOU CAPTURE THEIR HEARTS

8

ORGANIZING THE GROUP

WHILE I'VE BEEN PROMOTING the concept that a small group is an organism that must be free to flow and grow and multiply, there must be some organization that supports the organism. If there isn't, the organism might run rampant, grow without boundaries, and choke itself to death. It is the responsibility of the small-group leader to organize and to create an environment in each small group where the organism of redemptive community can flourish.

One of my wife's greatest pleasures is the flowers she plants in our backyard. When guests pass through the gate, they're astounded by the array of colors that decorate that quarter acre. You would think, since God is the great Gardener, He wouldn't need to involve anyone else to protect, nurture, and oversee His foliage. Yet, I keep finding bills from some gentleman who sprays our plants for us. We also financially support landscapers who plant our trees and dig our flowerbeds. My beautiful wife spends hours nurturing all that greenery. She'll come in from the yard sunburned and dirty with scraped knees and an aching back from all the hours she's spent pruning the plants and digging up vile weeds.

Plants will grow without any assistance, but if they're going to flourish and continue to take people's breath away, there must be a group of people with special skills, doing what they do best so that the right environment for those plants is created, protected, and preserved. This organization allows the plants to breathe, live, and reproduce. The same idea applies to small groups. Small-group leaders must build, organize, and oversee a team of people from their own group who will keep the environment right for the members to grow and take people's breath away

KEY AREAS OF ORGANIZATION

It's impossible to put together the right leadership team until you know what you're putting the team together to do. There are six primary areas that need to be organized:

1. SMALL-GROUP MEETING TIME
You'll need people who are willing to lead Bible study, prepare food (all great small groups eat great food), oversee childcare, lead prayer times, prepare and open their homes for group meetings, and, in some group formats, lead the group in worship.

2. DEVELOPMENT OF INDIVIDUAL GROUP MEMBERS
As the leader, a key focus for you will be assessing and planning for the development of each person in the group. This includes all dimensions of development, but especially spiritual and emotional. This topic is the focus of Section 3.

ASSESS AND DEVELOP EACH GROUP MEMBER

3. CAREGIVING
While it isn't necessary to have a person specifically designated to give care to the group members, it is important that no need go unmet. A small-group leader must continually be aware of the group member's needs. As needs arise, the leader must mobilize the time, talents, spiritual gifts, and resources within the group to meet those needs.

4. **EVANGELISM**

Evangelism must be one of the group's primary goals. Some groups do this in less aggressive ways than others, but you should be on a mission to help people find Jesus through the group. You'll need people willing to organize this aspect of the group's life together.

5. **REPRODUCTION**

Every small group should have as one of its objectives to produce a new group eventually. It's for this reason that wise leaders recruit an apprentice before the group has its first meeting. This apprentice will grow to be the new group's leader. Preparing and training future leaders is one of the duties of a small group.

PREPARE AND TRAIN FUTURE LEADERS

6. **OUTREACH**

Group that do missions work together have a much closer bond than groups that do not. Some groups find a widow or widower and take care of his or her lawn. Others spend a day working with the homeless or serving local social ministry organizations. Some groups actually go out of the country to do mission work together. If your small group chooses to do outreach together, you'll need someone to coordinate these efforts.

KEY GROUP ROLES

In *The Next Generation Leader: Essentials for Those Who Will Shape the Future*, Andy Stanley reveals the two best-kept secrets of leadership:

1) **THE LESS YOU DO, THE MORE YOU ACCOMPLISH.**
2) **THE LESS YOU DO, THE MORE YOU ENABLE OTHERS TO ACCOMPLISH.**

The small-group leader must know the group roles that need to be filled and fill those roles with the right people. These people become the leadership team for the group. Small-group leaders who give away responsibilities are giving group members the gifts of growth and fulfillment. Empower people in your group. They and your group will be better for it.

ENABLE PEOPLE TO GROW AND FIND FULFILLMENT

The roles and responsibilities noted below are essential for the success of your small-group ministry. You may choose to add others to this list, but having these roles filled is crucial.

SMALL-GROUP LEADER:
1. Build a leadership team.
2. Ensure the coordination of the group.
3. Meet with the leadership team once a month for planning and encouragement.
4. Call on the group as necessary to make certain no need goes unmet.

5. Recruit and prepare an apprentice to start a new group with some people from the initial group.
6. Be certain the group maintains an empty chair and works to fill it with someone in need of a relationship with Jesus.
7. Cast a vision for multiplication and begin the process.

APPRENTICE:
1. Prepare for future small-group leadership under the leader's mentoring.
2. Fill in for and support the group leader.

FACILITATOR:
1. Guide the group in transformational Bible study.
2. Develop a team responsible for creating subgroups of three to six members each.
3. Keep the group on task, but be sensitive when someone needs to share.
4. Subdivide the group, if necessary, for Bible study and deeper times of connection.
5. Emphasize the importance of filling the "empty chair."

CHILD CARE COORDINATOR:
1. Recruit someone to care for younger children.
2. Plan any special activities or training for children.
3. Select any necessary children's material.

HOST/HOSTESS:
1. Provide a clean home with enough space to subdivide into groups of three to six.
2. Coordinate refreshments.
3. Welcome guests and provide name tags at each meeting.
4. Ensure an environment conducive for sharing (e.g. no television, comfortable temperature, arrangements for children, pets, room set-up).

Jim Collins authored a celebrated book on leadership titled *Good to Great*. In his book he points out that any great endeavor is accomplished best when the right people are in the right place doing the right thing. He uses the analogy of a bus. He says to get the right people on the bus and then get them in the right seats. His point is to choose exceptional people to be a part of the organization you're leading (your small group) and then place them in the right seats (or roles). [11]

Some people are created to accomplish work others are not suited to do. So how do you place group members in the seat that's right for them? First, the group leader must discover each group member's spiritual gifts. Spiritual gifts are supernatural abilities the Holy Spirit gives each individual when he or she starts a relationship with Jesus. Next, the leader must identify each member's natural or learned abilities. Finally, the leader should uncover each person's passions. There are many assessments that a leader can use to discover this important information.

Once a leader knows this information, he or she can begin recruiting people to fill the right roles. Below you'll find a list of the roles that need to be filled as well as the ideal spiritual gifts, abilities, and passions that may be required for a given position. Please know even if you don't have people in your group who are perfect fit that the roles can be filled by people who are willing to carry out the tasks with God's help.

DISCOVER GIFTS IDENTIFY ABILITIES AND RESOURCES UNCOVER INDIVIDUAL PASSIONS

SMALL GROUP LEADER
Spiritual Gifts: Pastor/Shepherd, Leadership, Administration, Wisdom
Abilities: See and cast vision; humbly recruit and manage a team; lead strategic planning; shepherd people; model servant leadership; evaluate group objectives; and redirect the group as necessary to accomplish those objectives
Passion: Group members living as a redemptive community

APPRENTICE
Spiritual Gifts: Pastor/Shepherd, Leadership, Administration
Abilities: Willingness to be shaped by a mentor; see and cast vision; humbly recruit and manage a team; lead strategic planning; shepherd people; model servant leadership; evaluate group objectives; and redirect the group as necessary to accomplish those objectives
Passion: Group members living as a redemptive community

FACILITATOR
Spiritual Gifts: Teaching, Wisdom, Exhortation, Pastor/Shepherd
Abilities: Lead people in conversational Bible study; study and know what the Bible is saying; involve others in conversation; keep group members on task when involved in Bible study; ask questions that lead to heart and life transformation
Passion: Group members discovering and living the truth

CHILD CARE COORDINATOR
Spiritual Gifts: Administration, Helps, Encouragement
Abilities: Plan for the training of children; organize a systematic approach for childcare; recruit people to care for children
Passion: Care and nurture of children

HOST/HOSTESS
Spiritual Gifts: Hospitality
Abilities: Create a welcoming environment; help new attendees feel comfortable
Passion: Creating environments that reflect God's love

Once a small-group leader knows who will work best in a given role, he or she needs to seek a commitment from the person. It's always best to meet face-to-face with each person you are asking to take on a leadership role. Be certain you give them the following information when you meet with them:

FACE-TO-FACE ... ONE-ON-ONE

1. Explain why you think they are best suited to fill the responsibility, that is, what their matching spiritual gifts, abilities, and passions are.

_____
_____
_____

2. Describe the role they will be responsible for accomplishing.

_____
_____
_____

3. Explain how much time you believe it will take weekly to accomplish the role.

_____
_____
_____

4. If possible, detail the number of leadership team meetings they will need to attend monthly.

_____
_____
_____

Be sure to pray together. Tell the person you want to give time for prayer and that you'll call in a week to see what he or she has decided to do. After a week passes, call the person to see if he or she has decided to join your leadership team. If that person is unwilling or unable to take on this responsibility, see who else in the group may be capable and available. Repeat the process until you have someone to fill all the necessary positions.

NOTE: Some small-group leaders go through the recruiting process and find themselves unable to fill the roles that will make a group successful. If this happens to you, it may be necessary to meet with your group and share the dilemma. Explain that the group cannot be a great group without the right people stepping up to lead. Ask group members to pray about becoming a part of the leadership team. This discussion may uncover some people who were initially unwilling to become part of the team. You may also discover some willing members you might have overlooked.

THE RIGHT PEOPLE IN THE RIGHT PLACE DOING THE RIGHT THING!

9 CHAPTER

UNIFYING GROUP MEMBERS

ANY GROUP OF PEOPLE WHO ARE TRULY UNIFIED become a magnet for others. The human heart longs to experience oneness, so it makes sense that people dive headlong into a captivating collection of people who are really living life together. Not only that, a group of truly unified people accomplish enormous goals together. Individuals contribute sacrificially to the cause because they are energized by the synergy of the group and motivated by the deep relationships they've formed there.

BHAGS

The online Brainy Dictionary defines the word *unify* as, "To cause to be one; to make into a unit; to unite; to view as one." Creating an environment in which unity can be experienced is one of the key responsibilities of a small-group leader.

Unification of a small group happens at deep levels if the group works together to accomplish BHAGs. You're probably asking, "What's a BHAG?" It's a term coined by author Jim Collins—Big Hairy Audacious Goal. BHAGs differ according to the culture you're in, the kind of group you're leading, and even the doctrine of your church. This list illustrates some common small-group BHAGs:

GOING AFTER BIG HAIRY AUDACIOUS GOALS BUILDS UNITY

- Get together to pray for each other twice a week.
- Contact every family within two blocks of where the group meets to let them know we'd like to help them with any work they're doing on their house or yard.
- Go door to door in the subdivision where our group meets and ask if there's anything the group can pray about for them. If they welcome it, pray for them before leaving the porch. Do this twice a year.
- Members will verbalize any doubts they have about their faith whenever a doubt exists.
- Members will read the entire Bible in the upcoming year.
- Members will fast and pray for one group member one day a week. Do this for as many weeks as there are people in the group.
- Adopt the subdivision in which the group meets. Host special events in the subdivision on holidays with the goal of starting four new groups over the next 12 months in that particular subdivision.

In his fantastic work *Built to Last,* Jim Collins points out that great teams work towards accomplishing big hairy audacious goals or outlandish, spectacular objectives. When a small group decides together to pursue BHAGs, they experience a unity of purpose and passion as they work together to do whatever it takes to accomplish those goals. Interdependency, synergy, creativity, equality, accessibility, and grace are necessary to usher in this unity.

● INTERDEPENDENCY

Group members must understand the finish line cannot be crossed with a lone ranger mentality. Interdependent people are mature enough to realize they need others in order to make dreams become realities. Babies are dependent. They say, "Do it for me." Teenagers are independent. They say, "I can do it myself." But mature people with a passion for a mission are willing to live interdependently. They say, "You help me, and I'll help you."

SYNERGY

Synergy flows out of interdependency. Group members accept working together to accomplish their goals and realize they will achieve much more together than alone. There's an even greater depth of unity when members wholeheartedly embrace synergy.

CREATIVITY

Creativity is always a benefit but becomes essential as the group encounters roadblocks. For instance, if a small group has been inviting others to join the group but continually gets turned down, group members need to find a creative way to accomplish their goal. When people allow their creative juices to flow toward the same objective, unity fills the room.

EQUALITY

A group discovers equality in the process of synergy and focus on the goal. Reality eventually sets in and group members realize that their goals won't be accomplished unless each person is willing to do whatever it takes to make them happen. Suddenly the pecking order fades into the distance, the unwritten but imagined flow chart is deleted, and people sense they are *equals* with like voices and *equal* passions and responsibilities. When this happens, the group is experiencing unity.

THE REAL SECRET TO UNITY

Working to accomplish goals together alone won't produce meaningful levels of unity. In order for a small group to be unified, members must have accessibility to one another. They should covenant to be available to each other 24/7 if a need arises. It's in spending Friday nights together laughing uncontrollably, talking late into the night around a campfire, loving one another through the trials of life, and praying for one another when only God can meet the need at hand that the most intense levels of unity will be experienced. Making your group members aware that they can call on one another any time of the day or night sends a fantastic message. It tells each person that his or her group relationships are more than acquaintances. This knowledge alone unifies the group. Each time group members call on each other for a night out on the town or an evening of tears over the death of a friend, they experience deeper levels of unity.

SECRET TO UNITY IS 24/7 ACCESS

UNDERPINNINGS OF GRACE

Beware! Group unity won't happen until an atmosphere of grace exists within your group. There will certainly be disagreements and conflicts as members work together to accomplish their goals. When conflicts arise, high levels of unity are just around the corner, but grace must first be given and received.

CONFLICTS SHOULD BE STEPPING-STONES TO GRACE

As a preschooler, I cursed in front of my mother one day while my father was at work. It was a doozy, an expression that would make the toughest sailor proud! On the kid's scale of "punishment for things you should never say," this one zinged past sitting in a corner, washing a mouth out with soap, and a "mom spanking," and landed off the chart on "Wait till your father gets home!" Normally, my dad's return was something to celebrate. It usually meant a good wrestling match or a funny story from his past. But on this day, my father coming home marked the end of the world. I began to wish my father would never get home. Could it be that dad might get caught in traffic FOR THE REST OF HIS LIFE?!

Then I heard it! All the way upstairs and into my closet where I was hiding, I heard the front screen door and Dad's voice ringing out "I'm home, honey!" I heard his footsteps in the kitchen and then … silence. Silence can be the most penetrating sound on the planet. Then I heard footsteps coming up the stairs. Each step brought me nearer my greatest fear—a dad spanking! Those footsteps reached my hiding place, and the door opened. Suddenly, the face I feared to see was glaring right at me, but something was wrong. It was smiling. Dad was grinning from ear to ear, with his pointer finger signaling me to keep quiet. Glorious! Dad was giving me the universal "Don't let your mom know what's going on" sign! Instantly, I knew I was going to live. He took his belt off, but instead of giving me what I deserved, he began lashing my bedspread. In the process, he turned my way and chuckled, and I looked at him and laughed. He whispered, "Come on, squeal once in a while!"

Now this may not be an example of great parenting, but it is an example of great grace. You know what grace is? A dad who doesn't spank a deserving child. Grace is extra credit at the end of a lazy student's semester or a mother's hug after a haphazard spill. It's God's great gift of undeserved acceptance and love. When a small group looks into the eyes of someone who doesn't do life so well but still loves and accepts him, that group is operating in an environment of grace. Even though discipline and accountability are necessary, a grace-based environment is essential to the development of a unified small group.

In one of his sermons, Rick Warren, author of *The Purpose Driven Life*, said, "Matthew 18 is the story of the unforgiving servant. He owed $50,000 to his master. His master forgave him. He went out and found the guy that owed him $5 and strangled the guy because he wouldn't pay him. When the master heard about it he took the servant and said, 'If that's the way you want to play the game, OK. You're unforgiving; it will be unforgiven of you.' The Bible says we're to be merciful because God has given us so much mercy. The reason why I have to be patient with you is because God is patient with me. The reason you have to be patient with me is because God is patient with you. That's the way it goes. None of us gets what we deserve. If we did we wouldn't be here. It's all by God's grace."

As you lead your small group, you'll sometimes need to remind them of the Matthew 18 principle. When small-group members are sharing life together and working toward BHAGs, there will be mishaps, misgivings, and conflicts. Each of these should be a stepping stone to grace.

GRACE IS ESSENTIAL TO UNITY

10 CHAPTER

DIRECTING GROUP MEMBERS

CHINESE LEADER LI HUNG CHANG once said, "There are only three kinds of people in the world—those who are immovable, those who are movable, and those who move them." Leaders are those who can move people; they direct other people to greatness.

Throughout high school and college, I was involved in theater productions. I've played "Corndoggie" in a takeoff of the 1950s *Rock 'n Roll* and "Curly" in the classical musical *Oklahoma*. Both were lead roles, roles I was certain I could not do well. Memorization was (and still is) difficult for me, and I certainly didn't consider myself very talented. I had very little confidence in myself. However, I was willing to allow leaders who cared about my heart to direct my soul. Although my peers never knew it, I was an emotionally paralyzed person longing to have surgery done on my heart. These directors did just that. They believed in me, spent time with me, and helped me to believe in myself. It was through their gentle coaching that I came to discover a big part of who God created me to be. They empowered my confidence and helped to change the direction of my life.

I ALLOWED LEADERS WHO CARED ABOUT MY HEART TO DIRECT MY SOUL

INVESTING IN OTHER PEOPLE

Small-group leaders need to understand that many of the people they will lead don't believe in themselves. They need a leader who sees the potential in them and is willing to do what it takes to direct them to become all they were created to be. As I examine my relationships with these directors, I see that they followed certain steps to reach my heart and help me to uncover my God-given identity. I believe these steps need to be utilized by every group leader. When they are, that leader will create a team that's willing to follow him wherever the journey may take them.

STEP 1: SEE POTENTIAL IN EVERY GROUP MEMBER
Each of the directors in my story saw something in me I couldn't see in myself. The innate ability to uncover potential was within the makeup of their hearts. People who recognize potential in other people believe that people are good. They know that every individual has God-given abilities to offer the Kingdom and the world, and that people long to invest themselves in something more than the daily grind. Finally, these leaders find fulfillment seeing others accomplish great things. Ask God to let you see people as he does.

INVITE PEOPLE INTO THE LARGER STORY!

STEP 2: BUILD MEANINGFUL RELATIONSHIPS WITH EVERY GROUP MEMBER
Every one of my theatrical directors did more than spend time with me at rehearsals and performances. These masterful mentors opened their homes and hearts to me. They built relationships with me that opened my ears and my mind to the potential they saw lying dormant in my soul.

Leaders need to be certain they do more than accomplishing work alongside their small-group members. Enjoy times of recreation together to create bonds that can't be formed in a meeting. Get to know group members though conversation. Discuss interests and hobbies, debate the current events, and get to know what's inside. Get to know the diverse and sometimes perplexing complexity of people's journeys.

The greatest gift my directors gave me was familial. They opened their homes to me and made me part of their families. When someone welcomes you into his or her home, you enter into a place of safety. One of the greatest honors a small-group member will experience is being welcomed into a leader's home. When you open your door to a member of your group (other than meeting times) so you can just enjoy one another, you're expressing, "I like you enough to make you part of my family." When that happens, a leader becomes more than a guide or a director. He becomes a legend.

I LIKE YOU ENOUGH TO MAKE YOU PART OF MY FAMILY

STEP 3: **REVEAL THE POTENTIAL IN EACH GROUP MEMBER**

Once a leader establishes a strong relationship with a group member—one that establishes that the leader is a person of sincerity and honesty—the leader can tell the member what he or she sees in that person that he may not see in himself. You are more apt to see your potential when someone you respect hands you the keys to your heart.

Most of us see our identities through a dark veil. We see only the roles we play that are directly in front of us. They are usually the roles of breadwinner, housekeeper, childrearer, friendship builder, and, for some, churchgoer. All of these roles are vital and, in most instances, essential. But everyone has at least one beautiful, life-giving, life-altering role for which God created him or her. Discovering that role gives a new and astounding reason to live and is another step toward a heart fully alive. It may be that they were made to lead worship, to counsel unwed pregnant mothers, to pray for the needs of the world, or to take care of the elderly couple living down the street.

> At my church there's a young man who is a fantastic editor. In fact, his present paying job is to edit resources for one of the largest Christian publishing companies in the world. But deep down there is an ache that doesn't seem to subside unless he's involved in his greatest passion: drama that drives people to Jesus. His heart comes alive when he's in a room writing words that reveal the story of Jesus or when he's on the stage portraying a role that helps others understand the heart of God. By discovering this role, he has felt the power of accomplishing something in a story more potent than his own small story.

ANOTHER STEP TOWARD A HEART FULLY ALIVE

Each of us needs to know what makes our hearts come alive. Many people need a small-group leader to help reveal these abilities to them. The small group can be the mirror for its members, reflecting who they really are—the way Jesus sees them.

EACH OF US NEEDS TO KNOW WHAT MAKES OUR HEARTS COME ALIVE

STEP 4: COACH GROUP MEMBERS TO REACH THEIR FULL POTENTIAL

Once people discover their potential, they need a guide to encourage, affirm, and redirect them. This, too, is a role great small-group leaders gladly accept. It isn't always possible for a leader to teach the skills required for growth in every area. But he or she can encourage, affirm, and redirect.

You may be wondering what it means to "redirect." Sometimes group members simply don't get it right. They have moral mishaps, create tension with others, or are working poorly. In these times, it is helpful for the leader to redirect the member.

For example, in theater there is something called the green room. In actuality, the green room doesn't have to be painted green, and it doesn't even have to be a room. It is simply a place where the cast gathers before each show. One summer my brother and I were involved in a summer stock production that ran for over 60 performances. Before every performance, the director would redirect many of us. He would point out what went awry the night before and tell each of us how we could improve our performance.

Great leaders redirect those they lead. They gently point out their members' weaknesses and discuss how they can improve in the future. They do this with the understanding that they are responsible for protecting the hearts of those they're redirecting.

Leaders should carefully follow this step-by-step process when they redirect:

1) Make the person aware of your love for and interest in him or her.
2) Tell him/her what he did well.
3) Point out what he/she can do better.
4) Tell him/her how he can do better.
5) Pray for and with the person being redirected.

A LEADERS' REDIRECTS MUST FLOW FROM A HEART OF LOVE

We are to speak the truth in love (Ephesians 4:15). When a leader's redirect flows from a heart of love, not a heart of disappointment, discouragement, or anger, the small-group member is willing to listen, learn, and respond by striving to improve in the future.

STEP 5: **EMPOWER GROUP MEMBERS TO FLOURISH**

Empowerment is a potent tool. Giving someone authority to do what he or she was created to do after adequate preparation is a life-altering conversation. Imagine that you've invested in your small-group members as described in this chapter. You've seen extraordinary potential in them, built meaningful relationships with them, and pointed out their abilities. You've given your time and wisdom affirming, encouraging, and redirecting them. Like a proud parent, you look back at who they were, see who they are now, and know that they are ready to make a difference in their new world. Now that's giving your life to something that is truly fulfilling!

GIVE YOUR LIFE TO SOMETHING TRULY FULFILLING

A powerful portrayal of great leadership is illustrated in the film *Glory*. The movie is based on the true story of the first African-American regiment to go into combat during the Civil War. A young Caucasian soldier is called upon to lead this group of ex-slaves with no battlefield experience and turn them into a fighting machine. The task is painstaking and excruciatingly difficult at times, but he doesn't give up. He sees potential in each of his men. They respond to his leadership, but not until he is willing to pay the price for them. At one point in the film, he delivered this announcement from the war department to his troops: "You men enlisted in this regiment with the understanding that you would be paid the regular wage of $13 a month. This morning I have been notified that since you are a colored regiment you will be paid $10 a month. Regiment, fall out to receive pay." At this point in the film, the yard becomes a ruckus milieu as angry, distressed voices bombastically express their disapproval. They are unwilling to take anything if they are not going to receive full pay. Suddenly, over and above the screaming, the sound of a gunshot echoes through the cold, damp air.

All eyes are fixed on the colonel. The viewer is led to believe there will be disciplinary action doled out to these soldiers for their defiance. Instead, this wise young leader holds up his own paycheck and says, "If you men will take no pay then none of us will!" He then rips his own monthly paycheck in half. A lone voice is heard over the crowd cheering, "Let's hear it for the Colonel!" and then the troops scream out their approval of the now powerful leader.

Leadership is defined by a leader's willingness to sacrifice for those whom he or she leads. A leader must believe in people who don't yet believe in themselves, to take the time to build future leaders, to stand firm on behalf of his or her team, and to do so with all diligence (Romans 12:8).

GREAT LEADERS SACRIFICE FOR THEIR PEOPLE

DESTINATION:COMMUNITY

SECTION THREE
STARTING A SMALL-GROUP MINISTRY

AROUND THE GLOBE small-group ministry is becoming known as the primary way to accomplish redemptive community. You're asking for trouble if you begin a small-group ministry because your pastor wants you to run a new program in your church, or because you're searching for a new way to beef up attendance, or because you want to make a few complainers happy. The only reason you'll want to take on something this challenging is because God has CALLED you to this work. What is a "calling"? My definition is "an undeniable, inescapable expectation placed on someone by God Himself." If you're going to lead a movement of this magnitude, you're going to need that depth of calling. Here's the formula for success that arises out of a depth of calling ...

PASSION + PURPOSE + PLANS + PERSEVERANCE = SUCCESS

Follow this eight-step PLAN to begin your small-group ministry.

1. Decide if a small-group ministry is right for your church.
2. Envision the vision.
3. Choose the types of groups you'll include.
4. Craft a purpose statement.
5. Plan for growth.
6. Obtain approval from the influencing church leadership.
7. Enlist the senior pastor to cast a church-wide vision.
8. Recruit Generation 1.

3 PERSONAL HEART ASSESSMENT

The longing you have to start a small-group ministry won't make that ministry effective. Over the last 40 plus years, thousands of churches have jumped on the small-group bandwagon only to be thrown off by a lack of understanding and purposeful preparation. Creating the right environment throughout the church, as well as in the hearts of the people involved, is time-consuming but crucial to the success of a small-group ministry.

You want to start this ministry for the right reasons. Take a few minutes to complete this personal heart assessment. Please rate yourself between one and ten in the areas listed below. One (1) means "I have no passion at all," and ten (10) means "I can't stop thinking and praying about this."

_____ I am "called" to start this ministry.
_____ I believe this is biblical, and I believe it's the right way to do church.
_____ I long to see our church living in authentic Christian community.
_____ I have a passion for people to be transformed.
_____ I want to see people far away from God begin a relationship with Him.
_____ I want to raise up leaders through our small-group ministry.

A DEFINITE MAYBE

If you realize you're lacking in some areas, don't sweat it. Ask God to make you passionate about small groups. Get together with people who are zealous about the small-group experience. Visit groups already meeting in your area, read and learn about small groups, meet with small-group pastors, and attend small-group conferences and seminars. Pursuing these things will increase your understanding and inspire you to move forward.

TIME TO STEP AWAY

However, if you discover after completing the above evaluation and pursuing some of the things mentioned in the paragraph above that your heart is not fully passionate about starting life-transforming small groups, it may be necessary for you to find someone else in your church to lead this ministry. A small-group ministry cannot flourish if it's simply a program. Small groups must be spearheaded by an individual who is so fired up about the ministry that his or her flames of anticipation and exhilaration are contagious.

STEP UP AND GO FOR IT!

If the fire's burning in you, then the steps in this section will give you a process to start a small-group ministry that pursues redemptive community. There are two important principles you need to embrace before you begin with the how-tos of small-group ministry: (1) you are responsible for a fluid organism, not a rigid organization, and (2) everyone involved in the ministry must have someone who is responsible for his or her ongoing growth. Bottom Line: Those starting this ministry must plan for the growth of individual members involved in the ministry as well as the nurture of the individual leaders called to lead the ministry.

11

DECIDE IF SMALL GROUPS ARE RIGHT FOR YOU

SOME CHURCHES ARE JUMPING on the small-group bandwagon without first considering whether or not joining this band might force the rest of their players to pack up their instruments and go home.

Jesus wisely warned, "But don't begin until you count the cost. For who would begin construction of a building without first calculating the cost to see if there is enough money to finish it? Otherwise, you might complete only the foundation before running out of money, and then everyone would laugh at you. They would say, 'There's the person who started that building and couldn't afford to finish it!'" (Luke 14:28-30, NLT)

LOOK BEFORE YOU LEAP

If Sunday School or Adult Bible Fellowship has driven your church for generations, you want to be sure that God is asking you to guide your church into a small-group ministry. God does call leaders to motivate significant change in order to reach each new generation. However, you don't want to do this on your own accord. Be certain God is in this challenging venture.

If your church is centered on Sunday School or Adult Bible Fellowships and you're called to create a small-group model, you have four models from which to choose. Read the following descriptions to see which model might be best for you.

A DUAL APPROACH MODEL

You could add pure small groups alongside your current Sunday School classes or Adult Bible Fellowship group. If done well, these two ministries effortlessly strengthen one another. Adult Bible Fellowship or Sunday School attendees invite one another to the small group they're attending and visa versa. Church members can then decide whether to be involved in one or both.

YOU COULD GIVE CHURCH MEMBERS A CHOICE

A LIFE GROUPS MODEL

Marry the principles and practices of small-group life and Sunday School life under the same title, uniting the two with shared values.

> Dr. Angus McKinley at Bellevue Baptist Church in Owensboro, Kentucky is a well-studied cell-church trainer. When he arrived at Bellevue, he found a strong Sunday School ministry but no small-group system. He applied small-group principles and practices to the existing Sunday School groups as well as the emerging home groups using a common language. He then began to transition the terminology being used to describe the healthy small-group practices into what the church now calls "Life Groups." Now, all of Bellevue's Life Groups hold the same values and speak the same language, regardless of whether they meet on or off-campus. Church members are given the choice of attending a Life Group at the time and place that best fits their needs.

YOU COULD PROVIDE DIRECTIONALLY UNIFIED FLEXIBILITY

A COMBINATION MODEL

Transition from using totally Sunday School principles and practices to include small-group principles and practices in your Sunday School classes. This can be a difficult process. The book *Making the Critical Connection: Combining the Best of Small-Group Dynamics with Sunday School* by Hal Mayer will be a powerful tool to use during that transition. It can be purchased at *www.SerendipityHouse.com*.

YOU COULD CREATE A SUNDAY SCHOOL HYBRID

FLAMINGO ROAD'S SUNDAY SCHOOL JOURNEY WITH HAL MAYER

As we transitioned our worship style to become more purpose-driven and seeker sensitive, we realized to move to effectiveness we needed more than a contemporary worship service. We needed a relational, process-driven strategy to accomplish our church purpose: "To honor God, by leading people to become fully devoted followers of Jesus Christ." This strategy had to become the driving force behind our education and small groups as well. Flamingo Road had decided its purpose and target (our community), yet as we approached our strategy we needed help. How could we move people from the community to become fully devoted followers of Jesus Christ?

We knew at FRC that we needed a simple strategy, understandable to everyone so they could navigate the process. The strategy needed a vehicle to carry it, and at Flamingo Road our vehicle is the hybrid system we developed. This system is an integration of Sunday School and small groups in the form of "Midsize Groups." The average group at FRC is 15–25 people but uses the relational dynamics of small groups within a Sunday School structure. FRC's Hybrid combines the "best of" what we saw in Sunday School and Home Cell Group formats. [12]

A HOME GROUPS MODEL

Transition your Sunday morning Sunday School classes to in-house small-group meetings throughout the week. Make sure you do your research before deciding on the model. It may take years for your church to make the full transition. There's significantly more difficulty in transitioning a church to home groups than in planting a new church using this model. If God isn't leading you in this direction, this model could well bring more distraction and devastation than transition and transformation to your church.

BE VERY CAUTIOUS BEFORE DECIDING ON A WHOLESALE TRANSITION

The first step to beginning a small-group ministry is simply to be certain that starting one is right for your church. If you know it's right, go for it with ...

PASSION

PURPOSE

PLANS

and PERSEVERANCE!

Be wise in choosing the most effective and sensible system for your church.

CHAPTER 12

ENVISION THE VISION

ONCE YOU KNOW that starting a small-group ministry is the right thing for your church, it's time for you to move to the second step and establish a vision for your ministry. You must clearly know what you want to accomplish through your small groups. This vision will govern your purpose statement, the types of groups you'll have, the organizational structure you'll use, and your long-range plans.

DESTINATION:COMMUNITY

VISION IS VITAL

I believe vision is an inescapable expectation from God to produce something that is visible only in the mind of a chosen leader. Vision is a mental image of what a chosen leader is responsible for making into a reality. Before you can move one step further in starting a small-group ministry, you must know what your vision is. Without a clear vision:

- ◉ **YOU WON'T KNOW WHAT IT IS YOU'RE SUPPOSED TO CREATE.** You'll be like a builder with no blueprint. You'll want to build something fantastic, but you won't know what it is you want to construct.
- ◉ **YOU WON'T BE ABLE TO FIND PEOPLE TO JOIN YOU IN YOUR WORK.** Effective leaders recruit the best to help make their vision a reality. People will join you if they share your vision and believe deeply in it.
- ◉ **YOU WON'T BE ABLE TO CREATE A STRATEGY.** Strategies are created to make a vision become a reality.
- ◉ **YOU WILL SOON BECOME PARALYZED BY YOUR OWN LACK OF PASSION.** Satan aggressively tries to dispose of leaders by causing them to lose heart in their God-given callings. However, he's restrained when someone has a solid vision of the head and heart.

A STRONG VISION HELPS TO RECRUIT LEADERS

There are many ways that you can discover your vision. Sometimes God will give the vision to you. This was so with Moses. God got his attention through the burning bush then told Moses precisely what His vision was, to see His chosen people in a *"land flowing with milk and honey."* Possibly God has already put a burning bush in your path and planted the vision for your small-group ministry in your heart. Maybe you're like Nehemiah. He heard of a great need, was emotionally overwhelmed by that need, fasted and prayed, and courageously moved forward to meet the need. Maybe God has shown you a need and that need has created a vision in you too intense to ignore. Most often your vision will grow out of an already established vision, the vision of your church leadership. You've been asked by the church leadership to start a small-group ministry and that ministry will be one aspect of the total church strategy. If this is the case, I suggest you work with the church leadership to discover what they want to accomplish through small groups in your church. You can build the vision around their expectations.

BE SURE TO CONSIDER THE OVERALL CHURCH VISION

If there really aren't any pre-established expectations and you are still baffled about how to determine a vision for your small-group ministry, maybe the following story will help.

My youngest son is a very talented musician. His dream was to become a masterful songwriter and musician. Living in Nashville and attending school with the kids of professional artists really established this desire in him. But before he could begin his ministry, he had to decide what he wanted to accomplish through his music. Did he want his music to ...

1. Help others enter into a relationship with Jesus?
2. Comfort people going through difficult times?
3. Raise up future generations of musicians?
4. Lead to deep relationships in the community of musicians?
5. Bring joy to people in nursing homes, orphanages, and other places of need?

My son had to establish his vision before he could move forward to fulfill his call.

WHAT DO WE WANT TO ACCOMPLISH?

It's the same for us. When we're determining the vision for our ministry, we have to answer similar questions. "What do we want to accomplish through our small-group ministry?" Do we want to use these groups to ...

- Help others enter into a relationship with Jesus?
- Comfort people who are going through difficult times?
- Raise up generations of spiritually mature Christ-followers?
- Enable Christ-followers to experience redemptive community?
- Serve other people and the communities in which we live?

MISSION

If you're still struggling with deciding your vision, it may help if you first establish your mission and target audience. Small groups are best used for six things:

1. Developing strong, mature Christ-followers.
2. Building authentic, redemptive Christian community.
3. Holding volunteer teams together.
4. Helping pre-Christians come into a relationship with Jesus.
5. Supporting one another through life's struggles.
6. Bringing healing to emotional pain.

Most churches find themselves doing well in some of these areas but not others. Take a minute to conclude the area or areas where your church is lacking. You may first want to start small groups to meet the most essential unmet needs in your church. Or, you may instead want to align with key church thrusts and strengths.

VISUAL VISION

Once the overall mission for your small-group ministry is established, it's time to begin painting a mental picture of this new ministry. This mental image will become the vision for your small groups. One way to begin the creative process is by asking yourself a few questions. As you answer each of these questions, close your eyes and visualize your response. Remember, in answering these questions you're imagining the small-group ministry that will become a reality.

ENVISION HOW YOUR DREAM WILL BECOME A REALITY

1. Where will these groups meet?

2. What age ranges will be included?

3. What will these groups do together outside of the meeting times?

4. How will individuals relate to one another outside of the meeting time?

5. Will they call one another, meet to get wise counsel from one another, pray together, and support one another?

6. What emotions will be evoked as groups of this type share life together?

7. How many people will be in each group?

8. How will these groups celebrate when God does something on behalf of the small group or an individual group member?

9. What will each individual in the group be expected to do to prepare for the next meeting?

10. What will the strategy be for attracting unbelievers to the group?

You should now have some snapshots in your mind that are your mental images of what it will look like for your small groups to share life together. Get a poster board or a piece of paper and draw what you've envisioned. Share this drawing with anyone you are inviting to be involved in your small-group ministry. This picture will help guide you as you decide your purpose statement, the types of groups you will have, the organizational structure you will use, and your long-range plans.

BE SURE TO CREATE A VISUAL REPRESENTATION OF YOUR VISION

13

CHOOSE THE TYPES OF GROUPS YOU'LL INCLUDE

IF ONE SIZE TRULY FITS ALL, then a one-size-fits-all shirt would roughly resemble a sack. A one-size-fits-all seat on an airplane would give us the space of at least four seats. A one-size-fits-all car would require about 62 seat adjustment controls. A one-size-fits-all shoe would make walking beyond difficult. Sports cars would look like SUVs, hats would cover many people's faces, and watches would slide off our arms. Just imagine one-size-fits-all dentures or eyeglasses!

Just as in these examples, there is no one-size-fits-all small group. Your groups will be unique based on your vision, purpose, the area in which you live, the specific people in your group, and a variety of other factors.

A LAUNCHING PAD

The third step in starting a small-group ministry is to decide the types of groups you'll include. In Bill Donahue's book *Leading Life-Changing Small Groups*, he describes five kinds of small groups. He mentions disciple-making groups, community groups, service groups, seeker groups, and support groups. I would add one other type of group to this list—healing groups. Healing groups are made up of people who come alongside one another to recognize and be released from the lies that Satan has imprinted on their hearts. Jesus quoted Isaiah 61:1 when He unveiled why He came to planet Earth in bodily form. He announced, *"The Spirit of the Sovereign Lord is on me because the Lord has anointed me to preach good news to the poor, He has sent me to bind up the brokenhearted, to proclaim freedom for the captives and release from darkness for the prisoners"* (NIV). It's God's desire for each of us to be free from the spiritual and emotional strongholds that Satan uses to hold us captive. Healing groups accomplish that purpose (see section 1, chapter 2).

HERE'S A REVIEW OF THE TYPES OF SMALL GROUPS FROM SECTION 2, CHAPTER 6 …

1. **Disciples-Making Groups** – for Christ-followers who want to develop spiritually.
2. **Community Groups** – for Christ-followers and pre-Christians who want to build in-depth relationships with others.
3. **Service Groups** – for Christ-followers and pre-Christians who are serving alongside one another in ministry (ushers, musical teams, leadership teams, outreach teams, and the like).
4. **Seeker Groups** – predominantly for pre-Christians who are dealing with questions before trusting their lives to Christ.
5. **Support Groups** – for Christ-followers and pre-Christians who are seeking support through personal difficulties.
6. **Healing Groups** – for Christ-followers and pre-Christians who need to be released from the lies and bondage that trap their hearts and can potentially ruin their lives. [13]

Many churches choose to have just one kind of small group that disciples, evangelizes, builds Christian community, supports people through difficult times, and works through the healing process with those who are in emotional bondage. You will certainly want to explore that possibility. Take a minute now to circle the group type or types you'll try to start in the near future.

START BY FINDING A NEED AND MEET THAT NEED

There are many kinds of groups out there. Start by finding a need and meet that need with a great group. The success of that group will give you the confidence and credibility you need to branch out into other kinds of groups.

CHAPTER 14

CAPTURE THE PURPOSE BEHIND YOUR PASSION

RICK WARREN'S BOOK The Purpose Driven Life *has sold more copies than any other Christian book in recent years. Why is Rick's book so popular? The answer is simple: until people know why they exist, they don't know what they are to effectively do. It's the same with ministry. Until a ministry knows why it exists, it will not know what it is to effectively accomplish.*

The fourth step in starting a small-group ministry is to create a purpose statement. A purpose statement gives everyone in the ministry a concrete understanding of why the ministry exists and what the ministry is to accomplish. People who don't know why they are involved in a ministry are never really passionate about it. Everyone involved in your small-group ministry needs to know the purpose behind your passion. A captivating purpose statement achieves this.

EVERYONE NEEDS TO KNOW THE PURPOSE BEHIND YOUR PASSION

A FEW FACTS ABOUT A PURPOSE STATEMENT:

◉ **IT MUST GET TO THE CORE OF YOUR SMALL-GROUP MINISTRY.**
Be certain the purpose statement doesn't try to say too much.

◉ **IT MUST BE SHORT ENOUGH TO BE EASILY MEMORIZED AND REMEMBERED.**
You'll want every person on the small-group team to be able to voice this statement without hesitation.

◉ **IT SHOULD BE IN THE VERNACULAR OF YOUR CHURCH AND/OR CULTURE.**

◉ **THE PURPOSE STATEMENT FOR YOUR SMALL-GROUP MINISTRY SHOULD COMPLEMENT YOUR CHURCH'S PURPOSE STATEMENT.**

When our Serendipity House team got together to create a purpose statement for Serendipity House in 2003, I had the honor of being at the meeting. If I had been the sole voice in that meeting, we would have been in deep trouble. My suggestion went something like this: *"We exist to help people gather in small groups of 4 to 12 where life-change can take place as people share life together in interdependent relationships. They share common possessions, purposes, experiences, and meals. They grow relationally and spiritually, igniting synergy with God's passion as they do all of this to the glory of God."* Luckily there were some much wiser people in the room. If I remember correctly, all of the points I mentioned a moment ago were represented in the final draft. However, in the end, we came up with this: *"We exist to transform individuals, churches, and cultures through authentic Christian community."* Lately, we've created a shorter, more compelling statement that defines who we are. It guides everything we write and publish. *"We are a group of people unwilling to settle for anything less than redemptive community."* I couldn't have memorized all of the statement I suggested, but I can repeat the new Serendipity House purpose statement without hesitation.

A purpose statement must communicate the big picture of the ministry while capturing the heart of its work. Your purpose statement should complement your church's mission statement. If the mission statement is "We exist to help undevoted people become fully devoted followers of Jesus Christ," you won't want your small group's mission statement to ignore that important declaration. You might even try to use some of the same verbiage by writing something like "We exist to help undevoted and devoted people know Jesus Christ and seek His Kingdom through authentic Christian community."

COMPLEMENT YOUR CHURCH MISSION STATEMENT

Your purpose statement is vitally important. It's the guiding force that keeps the work of your ministry on course. The purpose statement will be used to measure what can and can't be done, what is and isn't effective, and who will and who won't be leaders in your small-group ministry. Anytime someone at any level of leadership suggests doing something that doesn't focus on accomplishing the work of your small-group ministry, you refer to the purpose statement. Any time a leader is questioned for his leadership, you ask, "Was that individual working to accomplish what is stated in our purpose statement?" The purpose statement is the archer that points your ministry at dead center on the target. It must be aimed at the bull's-eye. Aim true!

Here's a step-by-step process for creating your purpose statement. This can be done by an individual or with a small group of leaders who understand the small-group space.

STEP 1: Pray.

DID I MENTION THE NEED TO PRAY?

STEP 2: Pray some more.

STEP 3: Review the vision for the small group's ministry. If possible, spend time revisiting the drawing of your vision. Write down key words or phrases that depict the emotions you feel when you remember the vision for the ministry you're starting.

STEP 4: Make a list stating what you hope to accomplish in the life of every person who is in one of your small groups. Hone this list down to no more than three things. Discuss which of these three things depicts most perfectly what you want your groups to do. Make that the focus of your purpose statement.

STEP 5: Write a one-sentence statement that resonates with passion, purpose, and productivity. Your purpose statement might start with one of the phrases below:
Helping people …
Guiding people to …
Freeing people from …
Connecting people to …
Building people up so they can …

Writing your purpose statement is like drawing a bull's-eye on an archer's target. Without it, the archer may know there's a target to shoot at, but will never know how to score the most points. You'll want to take your time, involve your heart, and create a purpose statement that will compel everyone involved in the small-group ministry to do everything in his or her power to hit the bull's-eye.

COMPEL EVERYONE TO AIM FOR THE BULL'S-EYE

15

PLAN FOR GROWTH

HAVE YOU EVER DRIVEN through the state of Florida? My family and I did a few years ago, and it's a beautiful drive. As we made our way down the highway, we saw an alien-looking growth jacketing everything in its path. I later found out this plant is called kudzu. It engulfs full-grown trees and shrubs as well as anything else that gets in its path. I thought this aggressive vegetation was pretty impressive until I found out it is almost impossible to stop its growth. It can be managed, but it can't be stopped.

If you create the right environment for your small groups, your ministry will grow like kudzu. You won't be able to stop it. The good news is that you won't want to, but you will need to manage it. A well-managed small-group ministry will remain effective as it grows and develops.

CONSISTENT MULTIPLICATION

Don't get me wrong. Not every small group ministry grows like kudzu. But if your groups are living in authentic Christian community and welcoming new people into that environment, your ministry will experience numeric growth as your groups consistently and strategically multiply.

IF YOUR GROUPS LIVE IN AUTHENTIC COMMUNITY, YOU WILL SEE GROWTH

You need to be prepared for growth. Make sure you have a structure in place so that someone is mentoring every individual and someone is managing every small group. Fortunately, God gave us an example of this exact structure generations ago. It is referred to as the Jethro Principle.

In Exodus, Moses is leading this huge group of Israelites, over 3 million, out of Egypt. When he becomes overwhelmed with the huge leadership responsibility he's handling, Moses gets a little guidance from his father-in-law. Jethro instructs Moses ...

"What you're doing is not good .... You will certainly wear out both yourself and these people who are with you, because the task is too heavy for you. You can't do it alone. Now listen to me; I will give you some advice, and God be with you. You be the one to represent the people before God and bring their cases to him. Instruct them about the statutes and laws, and teach them the way to live and what they must do. But you should select from all the people able men, God-fearing, trustworthy, and hating bribes. Place them over the people as officials over thousands, hundreds, fifties, and tens. They should judge the people at all times. Then they can bring you every important case but judge every minor case themselves. In this way you will make lighten your load, and they will bear it with you. If you do this, and God so directs you, you will be able to endure, and also all these people will be able to go home satisfied." Moses listened to his father-in-law and did everything he said. So Moses chose able men from all Israel and made them leaders over the people as officials over thousands, hundreds, fifties, and tens. They judged the people at all times; the hard cases they would bring to Moses, but every minor case they would judge themselves. Then Moses said goodbye to his father-in-law, and he journeyed to his own land" (Exodus 18:17-27).

It's almost as if Jethro was a hired consultant. But you know what? The information Jethro gave Moses would have been worth the consulting fee. Without this wise guidance from Jethro, Moses' approach would never have been effective. Jethro suggests that Moses organize his group into a four-level organization with four mentoring or leadership levels (1,000, 100, 50, and 10).

TWO LEVELS

In the early stages of your group ministry, you'll need a two-level organization. This structure includes up to five small-group leaders who are each leading 10-member groups (five small groups of 10 equals a total of 50 people). You, as the overall ministry leader, will be responsible for the ongoing mentoring of each of these small-group leaders. You will also be responsible for overseeing the five small groups.

TWO-LEVEL MENTORING

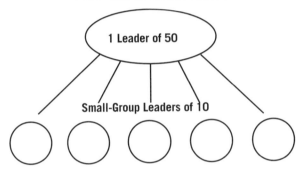

THREE LEVELS

When the initial five groups multiply, it becomes impossible for the leader of 50 to effectively mentor and manage the number of people and groups that are now in place. The leadership structure must expand. Three levels of leadership are required when there's a minimum of 10 small groups. This structure includes 10 small-group leaders each leading a group (10 groups of 10 equals 100 people). You now need at least two "Leader of 50s" who are each responsible for mentoring up to five small-group leaders and shepherding five small groups. You, as the overall ministry leader, will step up and mentor the Shepherds or Leaders of 50s and help them manage their small groups.

THREE-LEVEL MENTORING

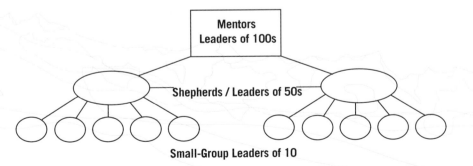

FOUR LEVELS

The three-level structure will be effective until growth occurs again. Then you must create a fourth level of leadership. As the responsibilities of the main small-group ministry leader become too much for a part-time volunteer, he or she must become a paid staff member. In the majority of situations, this takes place when the small-group ministry grows beyond 20 small groups. It almost always occurs by the time there are 50 small groups. You now recruit more Shepherds to lead 50s and Mentors to oversee the Shepherds. You then assume the role of Ministry Director as the Leader of 1,000s.

FOUR-LEVEL MENTORING

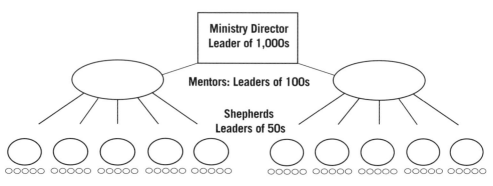

Ministry Director
Leader of 1,000s

Mentors: Leaders of 100s

Shepherds
Leaders of 50s

Small-Group Leaders of 10s

Ideally, each leader should be mentored by the person above them on the flow chart. This will keep the ministry from being without a leader in any given key role.

EVERY LEADER SHOULD BE MENTORED
EVERY GROUP NEEDS A LEADER AND A SHEPHERD

Because small groups multiply and should not exceed 12 people (or they won't be considered "small" anymore), we are obligated to be prepared for growth. If we aren't prepared, we'll find ourselves sitting in our offices, scratching our heads, wondering what we're going to do with all the people. From the beginning, think about organizing and preparing for growth.

IF YOU BUILD IT, THEY WILL COME ...

CHAPTER 16

OBTAIN APPROVAL FROM THE INFLUENCING CHURCH LEADERSHIP

THE NEXT STEP IN STARTING a small-group ministry is to get approval for the ministry from the church leadership. You may be thinking, "Shouldn't this have been the first step? Why would I go through all that I have gone through if I wasn't going to be able to get the necessary approval?" Listen closely … unless you complete the first five steps, you may not get the approval of your church leadership. I don't know about you, but whenever I've taken a new idea to church leadership, I've been asked a lot of questions. If I haven't considered the answers to the questions that might arise before I present the idea, I'm giving the impression that I really haven't considered all of the implications of my suggestion. Remember, you only get one chance to make a good first impression.

If you've covered the bases highlighted in steps 1 through 5, you're ready to get the key leaders in your church to meet with you. This first conversation is vital. If this individual isn't in agreement, you will be unable to move forward. You need the key leader in your church to join you in this if your small-group ministry is going to become all it should and can become.

YOU NEED THE KEY LEADERSHIP ON BOARD

Once the key leaders in your church catches your vision for this ministry, ask your pastor if you can join him and the key leadership team of your church to share what God is asking you to do. Be sure to share the following information:

- How this ministry fits into the purposes or vision of the church.
- Your vision for the ministry.
- Why you believe this ministry is important for this church.
- The implementation plan you will use to get this ministry up and running.

Answer any questions the leadership may have and write down any questions they ask that you can't answer. Consult a book on small groups or call someone in the know to find the answers to the questions. Once you have the answers, join the leadership when they meet again to give them the answers you've discovered.

Once these key leaders are on board, you're ready to go public with this ministry. The person with the greatest amount of influence now gives voice and explanation to the ongoing preparation and consultation of the new small-group ministry.

PERSON WITH GREATEST INFLUENCE IS YOUR VOICE

As you can see, it's going to take time to get this ministry off the ground. Getting to the point where you approach the church leadership for approval may have taken months of preparation. You'll want to remember what my good friend Pastor Brad Johnson once told me, "Too many people overestimate what they can do in a year and underestimate what they can do in 10."

IT'S GOING TO TAKE TIME TO LAUNCH WELL

17

ENLIST THE SENIOR PASTOR TO CAST VISION

WHEN [JESUS] HAD FINISHED SPEAKING, He said to Simon, "Put out into deep water and let down your nets for a catch."

"Master," Simon replied, "we've worked hard all night long and caught nothing! But at Your word, I'll let down the nets."

When they did this, they caught a great number of fish, and their nets began to tear. So they signaled to their partners in the other boat to come and help them; they came and filled both boats so full that they began to sink. When Simon Peter saw this, he fell at Jesus' knees and said, "Go away from me, because I'm a sinful man, Lord!" For he and all those with him were amazed at the catch of fish they took, and so were James and John, Zebedee's sons, who were Simon's partners.

"Don't be afraid," Jesus told Simon. "From now on you will be catching people!"

Luke 5:4-10

CAST WELL!

Just as in the story from Luke 5, if we cast our nets where Jesus points us, only then will we see the amazing results He intends. Follow Jesus' direction and focus on casting well.

The seventh step in beginning a small-group ministry is to have the senior pastor explain the vision for the ministry to the church body.

If you're a church staff member, key leader, or lay person in the church, you may be asking why the one chosen to cast the vision for small groups in your church should be the senior leader when God gave the vision to you. You brought the concept to the key leader in the first place, and you're the one who has spent the time laying the groundwork for the ministry. It isn't egotistical for you to ask these questions. In fact, it seems downright practical for you to be the one who steps onto the pitcher's mound and throws this concept toward the congregation. It is practical, but it isn't as successful. For some reason, God created a church leadership hierarchy that gives some leaders more influence than others. Because of this (and barring any unusual circumstances), the key leader has the greatest impact on the people in the church and needs to cast the vision for any new ministry idea in order for it to be seen as a viable option to church members. You may want the pastor to cast the vision and then invite you step up to the plate to answer any questions that may arise.

THE KEY LEADER HAS THE GREATEST IMPACT

This can best be done when the pastor is preaching a series of sermons on Christian community and/or fellowship. Some possible passages that might be communicated are Acts 2:42-47; 1 Corinthians 12–14; Hebrews 10:24-25; 2 Timothy 2:2; James 5:16; and John 17:9-11. During this series of sermons, it would be valuable for the pastor to talk about the new ministry that is going to begin soon and explain how biblical principles are at the heart of this ministry. It will also be valuable to describe what the positive outcomes of the ministry will be for church attendees and how people will be able to get involved in the future. It's important for the pastor to mention that you will be overseeing this ministry. Finally, the pastor should passionately communicate to the church what piece this ministry will fill in your church-life puzzle.

18 CHAPTER

RECRUIT GENERATION 1

THE FINAL STEP IN BEGINNING a small-group ministry is to recruit your first generation group. Generation 1 (what I will call G1 from this point on) will dream the small-group dream with you. Years from now, you will look back at what you have accomplished together, reminisce, and celebrate what God has done through the G1 team. This will probably be one of the most satisfying times in your whole ministry life.

Generation 1 is the first group of people that will compose your model group. You will lead this group. It is important that you understand the importance of this team. The term "cell group" is often used when discussing small groups. While cell groups and small groups are not exactly the same thing, the cell concept is a great way to remember the importance of this first group. It's like a biological cell that multiplies. The cell that comes from that original cell is an exact replica of the cell from which it came. Your future small-group leaders will naturally replicate in their own groups what they see modeled in the G1 group. Every small group that forms in the future will strive to emulate your G1 group.

AN ACCELERATED LAUNCH

The future of your ministry rides on the effectiveness of your first group. A G1 group is the ideal way to kick off your ministry if you have the time. For maximum impact, you'll want your G1 group to be a Turbo Group. Every person in a Turbo Group is a future small-group leader. When these individuals complete their time in the model G1 group, each will start his or her own group. If you need to accelerate this process, I'd suggest two Serendipity House resources designed to meet this need:

1. *Small-Group Kickoff Retreat*: This resource will jump start and accelerate the training of your small-group leaders in a single nine-hour retreat.

2. *Great Beginnings*: This six-session study helps to accelerate the understanding and experience of community within any small group.

SUGGESTIONS FOR RECRUITING YOUR G1 GROUP

PRAY **for God to guide you to the individuals and couples who should join your group.**

When Jesus chose the 12 disciples who would influence the world, He spent all night asking God to guide Him to the right people. "During those days He went out to the mountain to pray and spent all night in prayer to God. When daylight came, He summoned His disciples, and He chose 12 of them—He also named them apostles" (Luke 6:12-13).

Prayer will open your mind and your heart to hear God. Listen intently and allow Him to guide you to those who will serve Him best in this ministry. If you select any married people as leaders, look for ways to involve spouses as co-leaders. This is a great way to help the couple work side-by-side in ministry, and it's likely one spouse will complement the other.

SEEK **people with the appropriate spiritual gifts for leadership.**
Leaders with suitable spiritual gifts will guide their group members to become all they can become while accomplishing the group's goals. People with spiritual gifts of Leadership, Administration, and/or Shepherding tend to make good group leaders. Be aware, though, that God can use anyone He chooses to accomplish His work. Be open to other people.

CHOOSE **people who are passionate about the ministry.**
Choosing the right people to join this first generation group is essential. Your G1 leaders will become the models for every small-group leader that follows. They should have or be working to attain the following characteristics and abilities:

- A clear and explainable vision for the small group they are leading
- An ability to create a strategy to accomplish the vision

- The power to employ gifts and abilities of group members to accomplish the vision
- A capability to shepherd the people in his or her small group
- A willingness to be directed by those in authority
- The ability to lead the group to excellence in all aspects of group life
- The aptitude to model consistency, perseverance, sacrifice, and holy living
- A desire to raise up a future leader for the time when the group multiplies
- A passion to make the Bible the guide for life

INVITE **each individual personally to join your G1 group.**
A personal invitation is very important. Tell each potential member that God has led you to him or her after prayer and serious consideration. When you personally invite someone to join you, you create an instant and ongoing connection. The person is honored to be selected and knows you believe in, trust, and long to accomplish much alongside him or her. Jesus set the example when personally invited His disciples to join His team.

As [Jesus] was walking along the Sea of Galilee, He saw two brothers, Simon, who was called Peter, and his brother Andrew. They were casting a net into the sea, since they were fishermen. "Follow me," He told them, "and I will make you fish for people." Immediately they left their nets and followed Him. Matthew 4:18-20

SET EXPECTATIONS **by telling each person what will be required of him or her.**
People deserve the opportunity to count the cost before they join any initiative. Tell them the group goals, when the group will meet, what will be expected outside of the meeting time, what roles you may ask them to perform, and how much time will be required weekly. Also, be sure to let them know how long their commitment to the group will last. Because you're recruiting your G1 group, they need to know that you not only anticipate they'll be in the group you are leading, but that they will eventually be expected to lead a group of their own that will last at least one year. Allowing people to count the cost before they join your team will keep you from having multiple team members going AWOL.

Jesus was very straightforward when He spoke to those who were joining His team. He said, "For which of you, wanting to build a tower, doesn't first sit down and calculate the cost to see if he has enough to complete it? ... In the same way, therefore, every one of you who does not say good-bye to all his possessions cannot be My disciple" (Luke 14:28,33).

BE STRAIGHT UP

GIVE TIME **for each potential G1 member to pray about joining you in this small-group ministry.** A week would be appropriate.

SECURE **a confirmation of commitment.**

DESTINATION:COMMUNITY

SECTION FOUR
THE MODEL GROUP — LEADING G1

YOUR PRIMARY GOAL at this stage is to model great small-group leadership for the G1 group. Leadership is caught not taught. What you do in their presence as you lead the group is what your future leaders will do when they lead groups of their own. And clearly you can't take the leaders in your group on a journey that you're not on personally. Focus at least as much on living the adventure with Jesus as you do on training your future leaders.

4 BASIC INGREDIENTS

In an article for *Cell Church Magazine* titled "If I Could Do It All Over Again," Dave Buehring writes that he would be certain to include some essential basic ingredients in the creation of a prototype group. Those ingredients include ...

- A community that loves, cares, serves, allows members to move in their gifts and holds one another accountable.
- The application of God's Word to the group members' lives.
- A heart that actively reaches out to prodigals and unbelievers.
- The discipleship of each cell member as well as future cell leaders, and zone leaders.

He goes on to say, "I would now take more time with my initial cell. I would choose five or six other couples and walk with them closely for a full year until the Lord clearly gave us a green light to add others. We also needed to take on evangelism efforts and bring lost people to Christ and disciple them from the first day." [14]

If you can take the time, I would suggest you consider keeping your G1 group together between 12 and 18 months. It's important that this group live through all four of the stages a small group will experience. If these prototype group leaders do not experience all four of these stages, they will not know the difficulties, complexities, emotions, and obstacles they will encounter as their groups transition from stage to stage. Most importantly, they'll need to see an effective small-group leader help his or her group through each of these stages. It has been proven that it's very difficult to get a group of people to multiply unless they do so in the first two years they are together. Be careful not to keep your prototype group together longer than that amount of time. **For ideas on accelerating this process, see Section 3, Chapter 18.**

FOUR STAGES OF GROUP LIFE

Each healthy group will move through four stages as it matures. There is no prescribed time frame for moving through these stages because each group is unique.

BIRTH – Group members form relationships and begin to develop community.
GROWTH – Group members begin to care for one another as they mature as a group.
DEVELOP – Experience of God, Bible study, and shared community all deepen.
MULTIPLY – Group members pray about establishing new groups that begin the cycle again beginning with the Birth stage.

This section discusses principles and/or practices that need to be carried out in every small group. You'll want to be certain each of these principles and practices are foundational aspects of your prototype G1 group to set the stage for all the groups that follow.

19

FIVE ACTIONS OF HEALTHY SMALL GROUPS

"WHAT DO THESE THINGS DO?" the cocky freshman mockingly asked the professor who had brought a boa constrictor with her to the late afternoon Psychology 101 class. The professor responded, *"Whatever it intuitively does."* The 18-year-old jock glanced over his shoulder at his peers as if to say, *"Watch this."* Then, with a mischievous smirk, he sarcastically prodded, *"What if it doesn't want to do what its intuition tells it to do?"* Without changing her demeanor or turning to glance in his direction, the wise educator replied, *"It has no choice."*

WHAT DO THESE THINGS DO?

The primary question we need to ask about small groups is the same one the young freshman asked that afternoon, "What do these things do?" Is it possible for small groups to intuitively carry out certain practices? Are there group expectations and actions that float to the top when small-group concepts are placed in a jar and shaken? Some of the earliest New Testament small groups send us a picture postcard in Acts 2:42-47.

THE EARLY CHURCH GROUPS GIVE US A MODEL

Let me set the stage … Jesus has returned from the dead and ascended to heaven, the Holy Spirit has come and filled His followers, Peter has preached, and 3,000 people have become new followers of Christ. Many now realize that they have shared life with God Himself. The power of the resurrection and the Spirit has made them new creations and totally transformed their lives. In Acts 2:42-47, these new believers are simply doing what comes naturally as they allow God's Spirit to lead and fill them.

> They devoted themselves to the apostles' teaching, to the fellowship, to the breaking of bread, and to prayers. Then fear came over everyone, and many wonders and signs were performed through the apostles. Now all the believers were together and had everything in common. So they sold their possessions and property and distributed the proceeds to all, as anyone had a need. And every day they devoted themselves to meeting together in the temple complex and broke bread from house to house. They ate their food with gladness and simplicity of heart, praising God and having favor with all the people. And every day the Lord added to them those who were being saved (Act 2:42-47, emphasis added).

These verses contain a perfect model for what a G1 group should look like. The earliest Spirit-filled believers intuitively involved themselves in the following five activities.

◉ PROVOCATIVE, DEMANDING BIBLE STUDY

These new Christ-followers were hungry to know more of Jesus, His story, and His revolutionary teachings. They wanted to discover more of the larger story and learn from the apostles how to understand the Scriptures and their lives in view of that larger story and Jesus' identity. Wanting to understand what they really believed and how they related to God and others, these groups no doubt asked demanding questions and wrestled with the implications. Clearly, the focus was not on merely amassing knowledge, but on experiential Bible study that results in radical transformation. The first New Testament elder gave us this wise instruction, *"Do not merely listen to the word, and so deceive yourselves. Do what it says"* (James 1:22, NIV).

WE CAN DECEIVE OURSELVES THAT LEARNING IT IS THE SAME AS LIVING IT

⊝ REDEMPTIVE COMMUNITY

In the Book of Acts, 3,000 people found themselves almost instantly bound together. They gathered in small house groups daily. The community they experienced is beyond anything they've experienced in their neighborhood associations, clubs, and even families. These revolutionaries became intensely involved in a community in which the gospel of Jesus was being realized day-by-day in the lives of the "little Christs"—Christians—and those who were searching for release, good news, healing, freedom, hope (see Isaiah 61:1-3). They ate meals together daily, and sacrificed to meet the needs of others in the group. These small groups truly shared life together and shined light for people trapped in darkness.

⊝ RISKY, TRANSPARENT PRAYING

Prayer in Acts included tears of passion, expectation, and celebration. These believers were so in tune with one another's hearts, hurts, and needs that they not only say prayers, but they begged, pleaded, and prodded God with full confidence that He would act. These people grasped the awesome nature of God and yet were not hesitant about wrestling with Him. They stayed engaged when life became difficult and so experiencede dramatic movements of God. At Serendipity House, we've learned that God wants us to wrestle with the truth, so we like to pose tough questions of ourselves and of God that are not easily looked up in the Bible.

ALIVE PRAYER ... PASSION, EXPECTATION, CELEBRATION

"When they had prayed, the place where they were assembled was shaken, and they were all filled with the Holy Spirit and began to speak God's message with boldness" (Acts 4:31). After this experience with the Holy Spirit, their prayer lives were never the same. Peter prayed and Dorcas, who was stone cold dead, came back to life. "Then he called the saints and the widows and presented her alive" (Acts 9:41b). A group of believers prayed, and Peter, who was behind prison doors chained to two guards, was approached by an angel who set him free and guided him back through the city gates. "Then Peter came to himself and said, 'Now I know for certain that the Lord has sent His angel and rescued me from Herod's grasp and from al that the Jewish people expected'" (Acts 12:11).

⊝ DOING LIFE TOGETHER

There's a big difference between eating together and sharing a meal together. The same is true of living in the same space and truly sharing life together. To share a meal or do life together we need to slow down to experience life with intimate friends and family. Life is often shared around the table. In biblical times, meals could last a couple of hours. Eating together enabled relational intimacy. Discussions about Jesus' life, death, and resurrection and about God's work in the past were common during meal times. In Acts 2 the believers made life in community a daily priority.

WE NEED TO SLOW DOWN TO EXPERIENCE LIFE

⊖ TAKE CARE OF EACH OTHER

"So they sold their possessions and property and distributed the proceeds to all, as anyone had need" (Acts 2:45). You know you love someone when you will sacrifice what you've worked hard to attain in order to meet that person's needs. The early Christ-followers considered the needs of others as more important than their own. They voluntarily met the needs by selling possessions or giving from their storehouses. What must sacrifices of this nature do to the hearts of the people in any group? They would be unmistakably life-transforming! Winston Churchill captured this fact in his powerful statement, "We make a living by what we get; we make a life by what we give." Let's not forget the little things such as remembering birthdays, recording important dates—both good and bad—in people's lives, providing practical support, and giving the gift of our time and presence.

NOTE: The Bible clearly distinguishes between sacrificing to help others and enabling irresponsibility. Within the same discussion in his letter to the Galatians, Paul explains the need for wise balance: *"Carry one another's burdens; in this way you will fulfill the law of Christ. ... But each person should examine his own work ... each person will have to carry his own load"* (Galatians 6:2,4-5).

LOVE SACRIFICES TO MEET OTHERS' NEEDS

WHEN THESE FIVE ACTIONS ARE LIVED OUT IN THE LIFE OF A GROUP ... SOMETHING MIRACULOUS OCCURS!

The Bible is very specific about the result in the early church: *"And every day the Lord added to them those who were being saved"* (Acts 2:47b).

THIS IS COMPELLING COMMUNITY!

CHAPTER 20

THE ONE ANOTHERS

WHEN WE WERE TEENAGERS, we often silently asked ourselves the all-important question, *"What's appropriate in this situation?"* Wouldn't it have proven how brilliant our parents were if they'd given us a list that we could pull up on our iPods® that told us what to do in any given situation? Wouldn't it have been fantastic if we could've done a search for *"What to do when your date accidentally passes gas?"* or *"How to deal with a jerk who won't leave you alone?"* And, don't you think it would be tremendous if God had of list of what are appropriate activities between people who are in a small group together?

HOW THE ORGANISM WORKS

The good news is … God does have a list of specific actions that build true community and right relationships with each other. These are what the small-group world calls "the one anothers." You could search the Bible for the rest of your life and not find one particular place where this entire list exists. But, if you have some kind of Bible software program, you can do a word search and type in "one another." Your result will be a list of verses that reveal how we are to treat and respond to one aother.

Like the human body, the small-group organism is made up of many different living components. Each component has its own responsibilities. If not carried out, the organism will become ineffective and probably stop altogether. In order for the body to remain healthy, the components must allow blood to carry nutrients to each part of the body, and they must continue to reproduce cells in order for that particular component to stay alive and healthy. In comparison, the "one anothers" are necessities that must be carried out by each member of the small group so that the group can live in true Christian community and work together as the Body of Christ.

"ONE ANOTHERS" ARE NECESSITIES OF GROUP LIFE

The following story is a beautiful example of what it can look like when just a few of the "one anothers" are at work …

It was a beautiful autumn night. The group meeting was scheduled for 6:30, and it was now 6:40. All the group members were in their seats except for one: the group leader. The sound of his SUV in the driveway was followed by the noise of a door slamming and feet sprinting along the sidewalk. The front door flew open and the words "I'm sorry for being late. Things were crazy at work today" escaped from his lips. Suddenly this harried group leader realized that he had not prepared an opening discussion question for the group. Because they were composed of couples, the first question that came to his mind was "How's your marriage doing, really?" One couple, who had been married more than 29 years, affectionately announced, "Fine. No problems right now." Seated next to them was a young couple who had been experiencing naïve marital bliss for a full six months. The husband spoke first. With a flare of ecstasy in his young eyes that revealed his obvious bliss in the bedroom, he belted out one short but revealing phrase, "I LOVE MARRIED LIFE!" The leader abruptly thanked him for his comment and, with a good-natured grin, moved on to the next couple.

In his peripheral vision, he could see the obvious discomfort of the couple directly to his left. They had been married three years. They had asked for prayer a few times but had never gotten into any details. When it came time for them to answer, the husband spoke first. He began, "Our marriage is doing gre---," but, before he could articulate the word *great*, his wife shouted, "You know you asked me for a divorce last week!" The intensity of the young man's embarrassment and anger was immediately obvious. With teeth gritting, the red-faced spouse glared irately at his partner. God had opened the door for the "one anothers" to transform a derailed meeting into a life-giving, life-transforming, marriage-saving experience.

At this point, the leader set aside anything he had planned and allowed the group to help this distressed couple. He asked the couple to move their chairs to the center of the room. The furious husband blatantly refused to join the group in this experience. He knew what was coming. The group had before laid hands on and prayed for people in the center of the living room. With a little encouragement from a couple of the men in the group, both he and his wife were eventually seated next to one another in the center of the circle. The prayers that followed were heartfelt and personal. Tears flowed as group members asked God to rebuild this troubled marriage.

When the final prayer had been voiced, spiritual gifts were released as group members joined together to bring healing to this couple. A woman with the gift of mercy held the hurting young wife and allowed her to cry as she stroked her hair. Someone with the gift of teaching gently and naturally shared God's heart for troubled relationships from the Bible. A man with the gift of prophecy challenged the couple to understand what God was doing and to align with His purposes for their lives. And the leader, a man with the gift of shepherding, wisely suggested the men take the husband to another room to discuss his disappointments in the marriage while the ladies did the same with the young wife.

The young man told the group his frustrations. Dinner was seldom on time, and his wife wasn't as concerned with making herself beautiful as she had been when they were dating. The frequency of love-making wasn't what he'd anticipated. The group member who'd been married 29 years related the struggles and failures in his own marriage as well as the need for counseling in the past. He and the others assured the young husband that with work and God's help, he and his wife would get through this and become much stronger in the end.

A few doors down, the young wife informed the ladies of her dissatisfactions. Her husband came home each night and embraced the remote, but the thought of embracing her seemed to be the furthest thing from his mind (unless it led to sex). He didn't talk to her. In fact, he told her that since he's on the phone all day at work, he just doesn't feel like talking anymore when he gets home. On weekends, when they could be together, he spends most of the day on the golf course or watching sports on television. As a way to offer hope, the woman who had been married 29 years let her know these were normal troubles they could overcome.

Before the evening ended, the husband and wife understood their situation was not hopeless. They heard from couples who had also experienced marital difficulties and had overcome them. These couples became role models and encouraged them that their marriage could and should make it. Finally, the couple found a support group who would use their spiritual gifts and past experiences to help them through tough times.

This story is an example of the "one anothers" at work. The "one anothers" are some of the primary energy producers for the small-group organism. Did you notice that the group didn't need to do a study on the topic of marriage for this couple to get the help they needed? It was the integration of each person's story, spiritual gifts, sincere prayers, and honest, love-driven statements that brought the couple help, hope, and, ultimately, healing. The Bible explains some of the responsibilities of the "one anothers" in the verses below:

- **Carry each other's burdens** (Galatians 6:2a).
- **Each one should use whatever gift he has received to serve others** (1 Peter 4:10a).
- **Teach and admonish one another** (Colossians 3:16b).
- **Instruct one another** (Romans 15:14).
- **Speaking the truth in love** (Ephesians 4:15a).
- **Spur one another on toward love and good deeds** (Hebrews 10:24b).
- **Confess your sins to each other and pray for each other** (James 5:16a).
- **Submit to one another** (Ephesians 5:21a).

Make the principles below available to every group you ever start and every group member who becomes part of a group. Most certainly, instill these into the minds and hearts of your G1 group!

POST THESE ON THE REFRIGERATOR IN EVERY HOME

THE ONE ANOTHERS

- **LOVE ONE OTHER:**
  1. to demonstrate God's love (John 13:34-35; 5:12,17; Romans 12:10; 1 Thessalonians 4:9; 1 John 3:11,14,23; 4:7,11-12; 2 John 1:5; 1 Peter 1:22)
  2. to fulfill God's law (Romans 13:8)
  3. to increase our love for one another (2 Thessalonians 1:3)
  4. to overflow in love for one another (1 Thessalonians 3:12)
  5. to cover a multitude of sins (1 Peter 4:8)

- **CONNECT WITH ONE ANOTHER IN INTEGRITY:**
  1. to fellowship with one another (1 John 1:7)
  2. to forgive one another (Ephesians 4:32; Colossians 3:13)
  3. to greet one another with healthy touch (Romans 16:16; 1 Corinthians 16:20; 2 Corinthians 13:12; 1 Peter 5:14)
  4. to wait for one another to break bread (1 Corinthians 11:33)
  5. to help one another through difficult times (1 Corinthians 12:26)

SERVE ONE ANOTHER:

1. to use our spiritual gifts (1 Peter 4:10)
2. to love, releasing our freedom when necessary (Galatians 5:13)
3. to show kindness and pursue what is good for one another (1 Thessalonians 5:15)
4. to show concern for one another (1 Corinthians 12:25)
5. to carry one another's burdens (Galatians 6:2)
6. to show honor as you "wash one another's feet" (John 13:14)
7. to work with one another (1 Corinthians 3:9; 2 Corinthians 6:1)

TEACH ONE ANOTHER:

1. to teach and admonish one another (Colossians 3:16)
2. to instruct and model Jesus to one another (Romans 15:14)

ENCOURAGE ONE ANOTHER:

1. to encourage one another to avoid deception and live for Christ (Hebrews 3:13; 10:25)
2. to speak the truth to one another (Ephesians 4:25)
3. to lay down our lives for one another (1 John 3:16)
4. to spur one another on to love and good works (Hebrews 10:24)

BUILD UP ONE ANOTHER:

1. to strengthen one another in tough times (1 Thessalonians 4:18; 5:11)
2. to share a psalm, a teaching, a revelation, a language or tongue, or interpretation (1 Corinthians 14:26)

MEET ONE ANOTHER'S SPIRITUAL NEEDS:

1. to confess our sins one to another (James 5:16)
2. to pray for one another (James 5:16)

LIVE A LIFE OF HUMILITY TOWARD ONE ANOTHER:

1. to honor others above yourself (Romans 12:10)
2. to be in agreement or of the same mind one with each other (2 Corinthians 13:11; Romans 12:16; 15:5)
3. to not criticize or judge one another (Romans 14:13; James 4:11)
4. to not complain or speak badly of one another (James 5:9)
5. to submit to one another (Ephesians 5:21)
6. to be clothed with humility toward one another (1 Peter 5:5)

LIVE IN HARMONY WITH ONE ANOTHER:

1. to be patient with one another (Ephesians 4:2)
2. to live in peace one with another (Mark 9:50)
3. to accept and welcome one another with hospitality (Romans 15:7; 1 Peter 4:9)
4. to glorify God together (Romans 15:6)

YOU NEED TO BE THE MODEL!

In order for your group members to live these principles, they'll need to see a model of someone who is doing just that. You are that person. Group members follow leaders, and leaders lead by modeling. However, modeling isn't enough. There will be times when you'll need to coach and direct group members to live out these core actions of community. Don't hesitate to guide them down this path. When a small group fully embraces these principles, you'll experience life-changing, redemptive community.

21 CHAPTER

IN HIS G-R-I-P

INSIGHT ON THE IMPORTANCE OF INTIMATE RELATIONSHIPS FROM KING SOLOMON:

Two are better than one, because they have a good return for their work:
If one falls down, his friend can help him up.
But pity the man who falls and has no one to help him up!
Also, if two lie down together, they will keep warm.
But how can one keep warm alone?
Though one may be overpowered, two can defend themselves.
A cord of three strands is not quickly broken.

Ecclesiastes 4:9-12, NIV

GET A G-R-I-P ON YOUR GROUP

Each individual is uniquely designed to contribute to the small group. As people begin to know one another and become more and more willing to connect to each other's lives, there are four areas of opportunity every person in the group can give as a gift to one another: G = Spiritual Gifts; R = Resources; I = Individual Experiences; P = Passions. When these four areas are exercised, the unity of the group grows exponentially.

☉ SPIRITUAL GIFTS

God has given every believer a spiritual gift or multiple spiritual gifts. These are divine endowments and abilities given by God for the good of the others in the group. These gifts should be exercised openly and purposefully. When these gifts are utilized to work in the lives of others in the group, a unity of spirit is experienced. Each person finds a role to play that creates energy and a sense of fulfillment.

SPIRITUAL GIFTS WERE INTENDED TO BE USED

One evening at a small-group meeting, the wife of a seminary student spoke. She was eight months pregnant. She choked back tears as she announced to the group that she and her husband didn't have enough insurance to cover the cost of the birth of their son. They had been saving but were $750.00 short of the amount necessary to cover this important medical expense. She asked for prayer. The group prayed and asked God to miraculously provide the necessary funds. During the break time, the small-group leader was approached by one of the men in the group. The conversation went something like this:

Member: Don, I'm going to give that couple the money they need.
Leader: I appreciate what you want to do, but the group has had to help you financially on a few occasions. It wouldn't be great leadership if I bless you for this and then we have to bail you and your family out again next month.
Member: You don't understand.
Leader: I think I do. You want to spend what little money you have because your heart demands it of you. That's what the spiritual gift of giving does. It makes you want to meet everyone's needs. You need to think seriously about this before you give away your hard earned cash this time.
Member: Here's the deal ... You know that I'm really into golf.
Leader: I do. In fact I know that you save up so that you can get a round in once a month.
Member: That's right. What you don't know is that I've been saving for a while. I've always wanted a great set of golf clubs, so I've been keeping a few bucks here and a few bucks there. I've got $750.00 saved, and I'm going to give it to Bill and Sandy.
Leader: Okay, go for it!
Member: By the way, let me break the news to my wife before you make a big deal out of this.

When this man utilized his gift of giving, he not only met the need of the young family, but he also helped to create a dynamic that would last the lifetime of the group. It may be that your G1 group is not knowledgeable about the spiritual gifts found in the Bible. Key spiritual gifts are listed and defined below:

SPIRITUAL GIFTS LISTING

Spiritual Gifts, all supernaturally given by God, are His way of making sure no need goes unmet and everyone is effectively influencing those around them. Following is a fairly comprehensive list of gifts. However, not all churches agree on the list of gifts available to the church today. Check with your pastor, priest, or minister if you have questions.

SPIRITUAL GIFTS ENSURE EVERYONE IS ENGAGED IN GROUP LIFE

Apostleship: Ability to develop the foundation for new churches and/or ministries.

Distinguishing Between Spirits or Discernment: Ability to detect biblical misrepresentations, to make a distinction between right and wrong—good and evil.

Exhortation/Encouragement: Ability to reassure people who are discouraged, in need of counsel, or vacillating in their faith.

Evangelism: Ability to tell non-Christians about Jesus in such a way that they seriously consider starting an eternal relationship with Him.

Faith: Ability to believe fully in God's power and to trust God without hesitation to accomplish His promises.

Giving: Ability to give money and resources unselfishly to individuals in need and to the work of the church.

Healing: Ability to bring emotional, physical, and/or spiritual healing to individuals or groups of people.

Helps: Ability to joyfully accomplish practical tasks that support a ministry or person.

Hospitality: Ability to create an environment where people feel welcomed and honored.

Intercession: Ability to pray passionately for people/ministries with extraordinary results.

Leadership: Ability to obtain and retain followers and to organize, unify, and direct them to accomplish a God-given vision.

Managing/Administration: Ability to know how a ministry functions, create plans, and implement procedures that accomplish the goals of that ministry.

Mercy: Ability to joyfully meet the emotional and practical needs of those in suffering.

Miracles: Ability to make the presence and power of God known through being used to accomplish the miraculous in the name of Jesus (typically linked to prayer and faith gifts).

Prophecy: Ability to discern and boldly reveal truth that rebukes, corrects, and edifies Christ-followers, leading to life change and/or repentance.

Pastoring/Shepherding: Ability to cultivate, protect, and guide people to spiritual maturity.

Teaching: Ability to grasp the truth of God's Word, help others understand its meaning, and motivate them to apply what has been learned.

Wisdom: Ability to utilize and help others employ God's wisdom to meet a need or accomplish a task.

NOTE: The spiritual gifts listed below have raised a great deal of controversy in the church over the years with regard to definition and usage. Please seek counsel from your church leadership or Bible commentaries that you trust concerning the following gifts:

   - Tongues (or Languages)   - Interpretation of Tongues   - Knowledge

⊜ RESOURCES

The human heart longs for relationships that are intimate enough to have "Refrigerator Rights." Randy Frazee helps us understand this in his profound book *Making Room for Life*. He quotes therapist Will Miller as saying, "If you talk to any therapist today, the problems we see mostly are mood disorders: depression, anxiety, loneliness, and social detachment. As blessed as we are as Americans, as prosperous as we are, there's all this depression. So where is it coming from? I'm convinced it's rooted in the loss of 'refrigerator rights' relationships." Frazee goes on to say "A person with refrigerator rights is someone who can come into your home and feel comfortable going to your refrigerator to make a sandwich without your permission." [15]

People in our lives with refrigerator rights are the ones most apt to let us know they need our help, and they're the people to whom we feel connected enough to ask for assistance. We can't make it alone. We need one another. As you build your G1 group, make "Refrigerator Rights" relationships the goal. You'll find that when people in your group have "Refrigerator Rights," they're more willing to call upon one another to share resources.

"REFRIGERATOR RIGHTS" GET US BEYOND "HOW ARE YOU?"

There are three types of resources group members can share with one another.

1. SKILLS AND ABILITIES

It was a hot summer day. Our oldest son and his friend were in the garage getting ready to do what little boys do best ... build something amazing! I'm quite sure they hadn't decided what it was they were going to construct, but they were dreaming of something fantastic. I stepped into the garage just in time to overhear my five-year-old warn his young friend, "You better leave my mommy's tools alone." I'd always been a bit embarrassed about my inability to fix or build things, and that comment struck at the core of my inadequacy.

I'm not much of a handyman. It has been a humbling experience for me to allow people from our circle of friends to complete particular household tasks for me. However, I've noticed that the people sharing their skills always seem to find joy in the sharing of them. Through it all I've discovered that every member has abilities that others in the group don't possess.

When people use their skills to help others in the group, the Christian community that God anticipated begins to become a reality.

2. MONEY AND POSSESSIONS

Everything we have belongs to God. He gives us money and possessions because He loves us and promises to meet our needs. Another reason He gives us so much is so that we can meet the needs of others. For this reason, small-group members are responsible to give their possessions and finances to others in the group who are in need. When Luke describes the activities of the early church, he includes this statement, *"So they sold their possessions and property and distributed the proceeds to all, as anyone had a need"* (Acts 2:45). Just a few sentences below, he explains the outcome of this giving, *"... every day the Lord added to them those who were being saved"* (Acts 2:47). Giving away what is not ours in the first place (remember, everything is God's and simply on loan to us) brings joy. As my brother puts it, "It's always fun playing Santa Claus." When people outside the group see us giving away what, in many minds today, is the most precious thing in the world—money—they conclude that Jesus must be real.

IT'S ALWAYS FUN PLAYING SANTA CLAUS

3. TIME

For many, this is the most valuable resource of all. Until the discovery of electricity, life's rhythm came naturally, and part of that rhythm was time for relationships. Three activities filled people's lives: work, relationships, and sleep. Because the world was made up mostly of agrarian communities, people worked when sunlight was available. The average workday was from 6 a.m. to 6 p.m. Around 6 p.m. the family, and often the extended family and friends, would gather for a meal. This meal could last for a couple of hours as family members exchanged stories about their day, shared memories and past experiences, and laughed together. Conversation and togetherness continued until bedtime.

What I want you to notice is that there was a four-hour period six days a week that was set aside for relationships. Time is a precious thing. Unless every individual invests time in the group, it will never become a redemptive community. Ask your group to set aside time to be together more often than in a weekly meeting.

INDIVIDUAL EXPERIENCES

When people initially join your group, they will be hesitant, maybe even intimidated. They may think the people in your group have it all together. The truth is that everyone lives through distressing times. Group members can learn from each other's past experiences. Some people in the group may have experienced the aftermath of a miscarriage or the darkness of depression. There will most likely be someone who has been through the dark night of the soul, an era in a believer's life when God seems distant. God wants to use each group member's individual experiences to help others in the group through similar situations. Paul gives us some great guidance about this very thing when he sends this word to the church in Corinth, *"Praise be to the God and Father of our Lord Jesus Christ, the Father of compassion and the God of all comfort, who comforts us in all our troubles, so that we can comfort those in any trouble with the comfort we ourselves have received from God"* (2 Corinthians 1:3-4, NIV). It's important for each person in your group to look back at his or her life story, understand the situations in which God has been a comfort, and, when necessary, give the same kind of comfort to others in the group who are going through difficult experiences.

PASSIONS

God designed each of us with certain passions. Some people are passionate about social injustice, the Bible, children, people who are hurting, or prayer. It's important for group members to exercise their passions in the small group. When people in your group are free to pursue their God-given passions, unbelievers see people whose hearts are fully alive. A small group made up of people whose hearts are fully alive is a magnet for pre-Christians.

EACH JOURNEY HAS A PURPOSE

Be certain you let your group know that each of these four areas is vital to the group becoming a redemptive community. When possible, call your group members to action by utilizing their gifts and abilities in the lives of other group members. If you can get your G1 group to do this for one another, you will build a group with "Refrigerator Rights," and a group with "Refrigerator Rights" is a group far along on the journey to real Christian community.

HEARTS FULLY ALIVE ARE A MAGNET

CHAPTER 22

TEAM EVANGELISM

IN GRACIAS: A LATIN AMERICAN JOURNAL, *Henri Nouwen writes, "More and more, the desire grows in me simply to walk around, greet people, enter their homes, sit on their doorsteps, play ball, throw water, and be known as someone who wants to live with them. It is a privilege to have the time to practice this simple ministry of presence. Still, it is not as simple as it seems. My own desire to be useful, to do something significant, or to be part of some impressive project is so strong that soon my time is taken up by meetings, conferences, study groups, and workshops that prevent me from walking the streets. It is difficult not to have plans, not to organize people around an urgent cause, and not to feel that you are working directly for social progress. But I wonder more and more if the first thing shouldn't be to know people by name, to eat and drink with them, to listen to their stories and tell your own, and to let them know with words, handshakes, and hugs that you do not simply like them but you truly love them." [16]*

LET THE WORLD NOTICE!

In my opinion, there is no greater description of redemptive community than what Henri Nouwen described. In order for the unbelieving world to welcome the suggestion of a living, transforming Jesus, they must first see a group of people who know Him living in a way that we "know people by name ... eat and drink with them ... listen to their stories and tell your own, and ... let them know with words, handshakes, and hugs that [we] do not simply like them but [we] truly love them." When a small group lives this life in the presence of unbelievers, Christianity becomes more than a concept. It transforms into a living, breathing representation of the risen Jesus. It's the Kingdom of God in our midst.

SMALL GROUPS ... A LIVING, BREATHING REPRESENTATION OF JESUS

Small groups are one of the most effective ways we can reach an unbelieving humanity. We live in the post-Christian culture where people are unapologetically against believing the Bible is truth. People today are cynical about what they hear in a preacher's message, but they welcome dialogue on a given topic. They are willing to journey into the past because they understand that the past affects their present and future. They long for a few close relationships rather than a myriad of passive acquaintances. Small groups are the perfect environments in which people can experience Jesus as people in the group share life together. As we discussed in Section 1, Compelling Community is an extremely effective method for reaching the skeptical world in which we live.

COMPELLING COMMUNITY IS EXTREMELY EFFECTIVE IN EVANGELISM

So, how does a small group of Christians persuade someone to believe in Jesus, the only Person who can bridge the gap between them and God?

◒ PURSUE THE RIGHT PEOPLE

Start with the people God has already placed in your life. Think of those already in your sphere of influence at work, the grocery story, the ball field, or the gym. The list could go on and on. These people deserve a relationship with God, and they aren't in some foreign country. They are right outside your door.

People will come to your small group if you invite them. Dr. Thom Rainer, the president of LifeWay Christian Resources, polled people and discovered that they would be willing to hear about faith in a safe environment if simply invited. In fact, 8 out of 10 people polled said they would attend church if invited. You pass people every day who are just waiting for you and the members of your small group to welcome them into your circle.

Here are a few ideas that will help your group connect with the people around them:

- Do random acts of kindness in the neighborhood where your group meets. Mow the lawn, carry trash cans, fix broken downspouts, or watch a single mom's kids.
- Hold a block or subdivision party for the neighborhood where your group is meeting.
- Meet at Starbucks Coffee Company, Barnes and Noble Booksellers, or Panera Bread® Company where people other than church-types gather.
- Adopt a subdivision.

PEOPLE ACROSS THE STREET ARE YOUR MISSION FIELD

Eddie Mosley, the small-groups pastor at the First Baptist Church of Smyrna, Tennessee, has seen amazing growth in his group members and ministry. Some of his groups have chosen to adopt their subdivisions as their mission fields. In order to get new people into their groups, they host special neighborhood events on holidays like egg hunts around the Easter season. When you host multiple events in the subdivision where the group meets, you will encounter many people with whom you can naturally build friendships.

◉ BUILD RELATIONSHIPS WITH PEOPLE YOU WANT TO INVITE

Build relationships that could lead to an invitation to become part of the life of your group. Invest the time in building friendships first. Please don't misunderstand the intention of building this relationship. People should never be seen as the group's project. They must be viewed as equal partners in the journey to faith. The only difference is that they have not yet finalized their commitment to Christ.

FIRST INVEST IN PEOPLE ... INVITE LATER

Building a relationship with someone should be very natural. First, find out what activities you have in common. If you both golf, go golfing. If they're into shopping and you are too, go shopping. If they're movie buffs, catch a movie together. Secondly, invite them to your home for some relaxing, low-pressure activity. When you welcome people into your home, you communicate that you enjoy their company and would like to get to know them better. Play cards, watch a sporting event, and barbeque together. As the relationship develops, you'll naturally guide the conversation to deeper levels of communication.

◉ INVITE THE PERSON TO JOIN IN A NON-THREATENING ACTIVITY

At some point, when your small group is getting together for an activity that would not be intimidating to the individuals you're trying to reach, invite them. During the activity, look to see if the person you are getting to know is a "person of peace." A person of peace is prepared to hear about the Christian faith. When Jesus commissioned the 70 disciples to go ahead of Him to tell about the Kingdom of God, He gave them these directions,

"When you enter a house, first say, 'Peace to this house.' If a man of peace is there, your peace will rest on him; if not, it will return to you" (Luke 10:5-6, NIV). God will put you in contact with some individuals who are persons of peace the first day you meet them. But many people are willing to hear about Jesus only after they get to know His followers.

◉ INVITE THE PERSON TO YOUR GROUP MEETING

In time, if there's a connection between the group members and the unbeliever, an invitation to join the group for a meeting will be very natural. I'm often asked, "Should we be careful about our discussions when an unbeliever joins our group meeting?" Absolutely not! In fact, group transparency may be what introduces an unbeliever to the real Jesus. In his book *How to Lead a Great Cell Group Meeting So People Want to Come*, Joel Comiskey says, "Transparent sharing in the small group reveals to non-Christians that believers are indeed not perfect—just forgiven. One of Satan's chief tactics is legalistic deception, trying to convince people that God requires unreachable standards and that only 'good' people enter heaven. Small-group evangelism corrects that misconception. Open sharing gives unbelievers a new sense of hope as they realize Christians have weaknesses and struggles too." [17] He follows his statements with this word from Jay Firebaugh in *Cell Church Magazine*: "So when an unbeliever shows up in your cell, do everything the same (except pray silently that the Holy Spirit will reveal to the visitor his or her need for Jesus). If you carry on your gathering as usual, with Jesus in the midst of the group, the nonbelievers will witness the reality of a true relationship with Christ." [18]

SHOW PEOPLE THE REALITY OF YOUR LIVES AND RELATIONSHIPS WITH JESUS

◉ EXPLAIN HOW TO HAVE A RELATIONSHIP WITH JESUS

If the group is praying for a person, and he or she is seeing Jesus at work in the lives of the group members, there will, in most instances, come a time when it's right to tell that person how to receive Jesus' redemption. Don't miss this opportunity! Be prepared to tell people how you moved from knowing about Jesus to actually knowing Jesus Himself.

Take time right now to write down the names of five people you know who are not yet followers of Jesus. This list will be a great starting point for you and your G1 group.

_____   _____

_____   _____

_____

For people to begin a relationship with Christ, it will be necessary for them to first experience a relationship with you and your group. As you and your group share life together in the presence of pre-Christians, they will see the Holy Spirit in the way you relate to one another, pray and worship God, and invite Jesus into everyday life situations.

23 CHAPTER

COVENANTING

AS CHILDREN WE INSTINCTIVELY KNOW the safety of agreed upon expectations and the importance of commitments to keep those promises. This is reflected in the following conversation between Matt, an 11-year-old, and George, his younger brother:

Matt: "You swear?"
George: "I swear."
Matt: "You promise?"
George: "I promise."
Matt: "Cross your heart and hope to die?"
George: "Cross my heart and hope to die."
Matt: "You mean it?"
George: "I mean it."
Matt: "You're not lyin' are ya'?"
George: "No. I'm not lyin' or I wouldn't have sweared, promised, crossed my heart and hoped to die ... and meant it."

COVENANTS ARE BINDING

We are made for covenants. Even as children we know the safety of commitments to keep promises. The *American Heritage Dictionary* describes a covenant as "a formal binding agreement." Without formal, binding agreements, many people would never feel safe and secure enough to become involved with one another. Married couples covenant together when they pronounce their vows, businessmen covenant together when they sign legal documents, and loan-takers covenant with the bank to pay back all they have borrowed (plus a whole lot more in interest). In healthy small groups, every member agrees to some basic responsibilities and expectations in a formal group covenant.

FORMAL COVENANTS HELP UNIFY A GROUP

In biblical times covenants were so important that there was a ritual necessary to create a binding agreement. In *Cover the Bible*, Dr. Ralph W. Neighbour, Jr. describes how covenants were made in the time of Abraham. [19]

OLD TESTAMENT COVENANTS: SERIOUS BUSINESS

Step One: A sacrificial animal was halved, cut from nose to tail along the spine.
Step Two: The two halves were laid out on the ground, with the blood on the ground between the two halves.
Step Three: The two men stood facing each other upon the blood, with the halves of the animal on either side.
Step Four: They pledged their lives to each other.
Step Five: They committed all their wealth to each other.
Step Six: They exchanged belts and swords.
Step Seven: They named their relatives, each becoming personally responsible as a *goel* (kinsman-redeemer) for the relatives of the other person in the event of an untimely death.
Step Eight: They pledged their *hesed* ("godly grace" or "loving-kindness") to one another. This meant that they would remain committed to each other regardless of what evil deed the other might commit in the future.
Step Nine: They walked in a figure eight around the halved animal, so each man stood in the place of the other one at the end of the walk.
Step Ten: They cut their wrists with a knife, grasped hands, and mingled their dripping blood as a sign of their oath.
Step Eleven: They exchanged their very names, each adding to his own the name of the other person.
Step Twelve: They rubbed charcoal into their cuts, making them permanently visible to all.
Step Thirteen: Finally, they planted a tree upon the blood, to mark the place where the Covenant had been cut (made).

Although small groups don't really need to go to the extremes that Abraham and others did in the Old Testament, the principles are still true today. First, group members should pledge to share their lives with each other. Secondly, they should agree to meet one another's needs. Thirdly, group members need to commit to "loving-kindness." In other words, they need to give and receive grace. Finally, their agreements should be permanently visible to the world because, as Jesus said, *"By this all people will know that you are My disciples, if you have love for one another"* (John 13:35). Outsiders will judge your group's commitment to one another as they watch how you prove your love by the way you treat each other and meet each other's needs.

COMMIT TO RELATIONSHIPS FULL OF GRACE
LIVE VISIBLY AS A LIGHT TO THE WORLD

BENEFITS OF COVENANTS

Covenanting in small groups is essential. A covenant gets everyone to commit to equal levels of responsibility and activity in the group. Some benefits of a covenant are as follows:

- It provides the group with a vision and purpose.
- It becomes a roadmap to the destination of redemptive community.
- It establishes a framework for managing potential conflict.
- It creates healthy boundaries.
- It eliminates unspoken expectations.

MODEL OF A GROUP COVENANT

PRIORITY: While we are in this group, we will give the group meetings priority. (Prioritizing group time creates healthy levels of expectation.)

PARTICIPATION: Everyone participates and no one dominates. (Participating in group experiences unites the group.)

RESPECT: Everyone is given the right to his or her own opinions, and all questions are encouraged and respected. (Respecting others' opinions creates a safe group synergy.)

CONFIDENTIALITY: Anything said in our meetings is never repeated outside the meeting. (Keeping conversations confidential opens the door for healing as in James 5:16.)

LIFE CHANGE: We will regularly assess progress toward applying the truths we discover. We will complete any assignments and also strive to integrate what we've learned into our lives. (Our goal as a group should be life transformation, not the gathering of knowledge.)

CARE AND SUPPORT: Permission is given to call upon each other in a time of need—even in the middle of the night. The group will provide for every member. (Supporting one another is the only way to become a true community.)

ADVICE GIVING: Unsolicited advice is not allowed.(Protection from the excessive advice-giver protects community.)

EMPTY CHAIR: Our group will work together to fill the empty chair with an unchurched person. (Utilizing the empty chair gives the group a vision beyond the group.)

MISSION: We agree as a group to reach out and invite others to join us and to work toward the multiplication of our group to form new groups.

MINISTRY: We will encourage one another to volunteer to serve in ministry and to support missions by giving financially and/or personally serving.

FINALIZING YOUR GROUP COVENANT TOGETHER

Step 1: Share a completed covenant like the one above with the group.
Toward the end of a group meeting, give each member a copy of a completed covenant. Explain why a covenant is necessary by sharing some of the benefits discussed earlier in this chapter. Ask them to look over the covenant in the upcoming week. Tell them that the entire group will agree to the covenant before it's finalized.

Step 2: Discuss each aspect of the covenant.
When the group members return the next week, spend the time discussing each aspect of the covenant. When members are hesitant about points, ask them to clarify their concerns. Ask the group what they believe will be lost if this aspect of the covenant is modified.

Step 3: Work towards consensus.
You may need to discuss the covenant agreement for three or four weeks before finalizing it. It may be necessary to rewrite some aspects of the covenant. That's okay. Just don't alter the covenant so much that it will keep the group from accomplishing authentic redemptive community. The crucial parts include Participation, Confidentiality, Empty Chair, Support, Life Change, and Mission.

Step 4: All group members agree to live out the expectations of the group covenant.
Once all group members are in agreement, you have taken the first step to creating a safe and inviting environment. Many group leaders ask their group members to bring their copies of the covenant back to the group with their signatures on it. If you choose not to do this, you will want each individual in the group to at least publicly verbalize their commitment to live out the group covenant.

Covenants are not antiquated ways to make demands of the people in your group. Covenants are agreements that will keep your group on the right path as they journey together. Without an agreed upon covenant, your group may end up in the jungle of discontent, unresolved conflict, or overwhelming apathy.

STAY OUT OF THE JUNGLE

24

POWER PRAYER

RICHARD J. FOSTER, *author of* Prayer, Finding the Heart's True Home, *and* Celebration of Discipline, *aptly describes the state of many believers today. "We today yearn and hide from prayer. We are attracted to it and repelled by it. We believe prayer is something we should do, even something we want to do, but it seems like a chasm stands between us and actually praying. We experience the agony of prayerlessness."* [20]

INTEGRATING STORIES

When people pray, there is an integration of two great stories. The person praying tells his or her story to the One whose story makes prayer possible. And, as we pray, we are carried into the land of faith. It is there we find hope and help. It is there that we find our Narnia. Like Lucy in C.S. Lewis' *The Lion, the Witch, and the Wardrobe*, we must be willing to believe that in Narnia, on the other side of the wardrobe, Aslan (Jesus) is longing for us to request His help. If we do, He will involve Himself in our stories.

LEARNING TO PRAY

All too often, prayer is far less than a journey into hope and help. I believe the primary reason believers today are intimidated by prayer is that they haven't had the opportunity to learn to pray by seeing prayer modeled. Christians have been directed to hide in our prayer closets for a "Quiet Time." Some of us long to hear God speak during this time, but the truth is that we can't get the to-do list out of our minds. In fact, we end up asking God to bless our to-do list. Many of us have gone to seminars or read books about praying. We write down a list of ways to pray and things about which to pray. Some of us have even used these notes to preach better sermons on the topic of prayer. Yet, we still don't know how to pray. We need believers to model prayer for us.

When Jesus was asked by one of His disciples to teach them all to pray, He didn't give them a sermon to download onto their iPods® or send them to the local Christian bookstore to get the hottest book on the topic. He didn't get out His PowerPoint projector and point the laser pointer at a diagram on prayer. He prayed for them. He prayed while they listened in (Luke 11:1-4). People learn how to pray by listening while others pray.

One of the most vital roles small groups can play in the life of a Christian is to teach people to pray. Not only can group members hear prayer modeled, they can also pray themselves. Members should be given the opportunity to pray silently as long as they would like or to take steps into public praying at a time that is right for them. It should be made known to the pre-Christians in the group that they don't have to pray at all. They can simply listen in while the rest of the group prays.

There are two great fears people have when they come to a small group. One is that they'll have to read aloud, and the other is that they'll be expected to pray aloud. The group leader should alleviate those fears by having a progressive and systematic strategy in place to teach people how to pray.

The following five levels of increasing involvement will help your small group members learn to pray aloud:

⊜ **LEVEL ONE:** The leader prays and models conversational prayer for the others. The term "conversational" is important. Exhibiting a preacher voice, speaking in old English terms, or sounding as though you've swallowed a pile of "O Pity Me's" will only confuse the small-group member who longs to have an authentic relationship with Jesus.

⊜ **LEVEL TWO:** After conversational prayer has been modeled for a couple of weeks, the leader asks for prayer volunteers and sees who emerges.

⊜ **LEVEL THREE:** The leader calls on two volunteers to pray and then closes in prayer.

⊜ **LEVEL FOUR:** The leader leads the group to individually "Complete the Sentence." This could be a sentence like, "God, this is _____. I want to thank You for_____. or God, would You help with _____?" The leader lets members know that if they prefer to pray silently to God instead of aloud, they can let the group know by squeezing the hand of the person next to them or saying the word "Amen" to indicate they are going to pray silently.

⊜ **LEVEL FIVE:** The group grows to the place where they can pray conversationally as a group using this method. A prayer request is shared and the group spends time praying "sentence prayers" about that specific request before moving on to the next prayer request.

One of the greatest moments in my life of ministry came just a few months ago. One of the small-group leaders at our church was speaking with me about the growth he was seeing in his group members. I was already on the edge of my seat when he told me about one of the members who had prayed aloud for the very first time the week prior. My heart danced! As I drove home that day, the tears flowed because the man he was telling me about has a fantastic wife and two incredible sons. During my drive home that afternoon I realized that those young boys were going to grow up in a home where their father prayed for them, and they, in turn, would repeat what they saw their father do and pray with their own children. Because a small-group leader took the time to strategically train his small-group members to pray aloud, this family's legacy had been altered for generations to come. It doesn't get much better than that!

THE PRAYER EXPERIENCE

You want to be sure you teach the people in your G1 group to pray aloud by modeling it for them. If every one of them is already a prayer warrior, show them how to teach their future groups to pray. You will also want to teach your G1 group to lead corporate prayer. A great friend of mine, John Franklin, is an expert in the area of prayer. In his book *And the Place Was Shaken*, he gives some fantastic guidance to anyone who leads groups of people gathered to pray.

John's research in the New Testament points out that in most instances, the great movements of God came when Christ-followers prayed in groups. He goes on to explain the format that seems to be most prevalent. This includes the key elements we see in The Lord's Prayer (Matthew 6). [21]

- **FOCUS ON GOD:** You must start by focusing on God if the rest of the prayer time is to be God-centered. Ask your group to spend a few moments meditating on an aspect of God's character that is relevant to the group's present situation.
- **RESPOND FROM THE HEART:** When God's people truly focus on Him, their hearts respond. Encourage group members to respond to God by singing together to Him and thanking Him for the characteristic in focus.
- **SEEK FIRST THE KINGDOM:** Jesus taught His disciples to pray for the kingdom of God before asking for daily bread. Pray for the needs of God's work together at this time.
- **PRESENT YOUR REQUESTS:** Pray for the needs and concerns of the people in your group.
- **CLOSE IN CELEBRATION:** Offer prayers of thanksgiving and sing songs of celebration.

Obviously, if you chose to spend a large amount of time on any one of these areas, the group's prayer time could last an hour. Instead, make this a guided prayer time. That way you can let the group members know what the next phase of the prayer experience is. You'll need to keep each of these prayer times short and potent except for the time of presenting personal requests to God. Small-group members anticipate meaningful prayer time for one another when they come together.

The chart on the next page is adapted from *And The Place Was Shaken*. It will give you some creative ideas to incorporate into your various group meetings.

When believers pray together, phenomenal things happen. A group of believers were together praying in the Book of Acts, and here's what happened, *"When they had prayed, the place where they were assembled was shaken, and they were all filled with the Holy Spirit and began to speak God's message with boldness"* (Acts 4:31). These believers asked for boldness. They received it, and their world was shaken. Be sure to incorporate authentic small-group prayer into your meeting times.

TWO PILLARS OF A PRAYER EXPERIENCE [22]

GOD-CENTERED FORMAT
INVOLVEMENT ACTIVITIES

Focus on God

- Who He is
- What He can do
- His presence
- Getting His perspective

Respond from the heart

- In touch with feeling and deeply-held beliefs
- Exercising faith
- Honesty with God and self
- Repentance
- Dependence on God
- Praise

Seek first the Kingdom

- Pray for one another's spiritual walks
- Pray for the backslidden
- Pray for the lost
- Pray for missions
- Pray for awakening
- Pray for VBS

Present your requests

- Health
- Finances
- Jobs
- Family
- Other personal concerns

Close in celebration

- Thanksgiving
- Proclamation
- Praise
- Declaration

Focusing

- Leader's words
- Scripture
- Music
- Testimony
- Drama
- Group responses

Participation activities

- Ask people to have different roles in leading, testifying, and reading Scripture
- Singing
- Praying aloud all at once
- Responsive reading
- Large group sentence prayer
- Kneel
- Stand in pairs
- Go to someone else during the prayer time
- Write a prayer card note
- Prayer walk

Ministering activities

- Use a prayer chair
- Pray for focus groups in the church or community
- Pray for and bless one another by name

NOTES

CHAPTER 25

MULTIPLICATION

EVERY LIVING ORGANISM goes through a lifecycle that includes birth, growth, healthy of development, and death. Small groups experience this natural lifecycle with one major twist. The final phase is not the end for a small group, but a new beginning. When a group ends, it creates an opportunity to produce a new group and birth another generation of people who will pursue redemptive community. Just as in the growth cycle of any living organism, we call this process "multiplication."

WAYS TO MULTIPLY

There are three basic approaches to multiplying groups.

1. The present leader gets a new apprentice and starts a new group.

The present apprentice becomes the leader of the present group. The group continues having lost only the present leader.

2. The present apprentice becomes a small-group leader and leaves the present group to start a new one.

The present group can find great satisfaction in knowing they have been involved in the training of the apprentice.

3. The present apprentice and leader split the present small group in half and form two groups.

This is typically the most effective way to start a new group because the members have already experienced small-group life together. There is a meaningful bond between those who remain, but the new group is open to welcoming new people. Also, the core of the new group already knows and appreciates the heart of their small-group leader.

PAIN OF MULTIPLYING IS EASED BY A WISE APPROACH

Deciding who will go with the apprentice and who will remain with the present leader can be a painstaking process. However, the pain can be minimized if you utilize a wise approach and continue to focus on the positive opportunities in multiplying. Obviously, your goal is to have two healthy small groups, and the best way to have two healthy groups is to create two healthy teams. You will know you have two healthy teams if each team contains members with the necessary gifts and abilities for a fully functioning group. As you decide which group members will move to the apprentice's group and which will stay with the current leader, weigh the member's abilities and gifts and place them appropriately. If you have two people with the spiritual gift of hospitality, place these people in different groups. If you have someone with the gift of teaching and you know the group leader is weak in that area, put the person with the gift of teaching in that leader's group. Be sure to consider close friendships and individual preferences in the decision too; you want to minimize negative feelings in this transition. This placement method should be more art than science so it will honor each person and build two healthy groups.

PLACE PEOPLE ACCORDING TO GIFTS AND ABILITIES

PREPARATION IS VITAL

Anyone who has ever led a small group will tell you that the most difficult responsibility a small group has is multiplication. Your group will feel better about the expectation to multiply if they understand why they are being asked to make the change. There are three great reasons for a group to multiply.

THERE ARE 3 GREAT REASONS FOR GROUPS TO MULTIPLY

1. If a group remains together more than two years, it will most likely become stagnant.

2. If the group remains together and doesn't allow new people to join, the primary purposes of the group (helping others begin a relationship with Jesus and discipling believers at all levels of spiritual maturity) will be lost, as the group becomes a clique without a cause.

3. God never intended for groups of believers to close themselves off to those in need of a relationship with Him.

Occasionally, I've been asked to help groups understand the importance of multiplying. These groups have usually decided they have a great thing going, and they don't want to lose the relationships they are experiencing. I simply ask these groups two questions:

1. In human history, what group of 12 deserved to close down and never multiply? The immediate response is "Jesus' disciples." I then remind the group that the disciples had sat around the campfire with Jesus Himself, the greatest small-group Leader of all time, and listened to the wisdom that flowed from His lips.

2. What if the disciples had decided to stay together and never spread the news about Jesus? The response is always a deafening, uneasy silence. Usually someone will break the stillness and tell the group that they may need to consider multiplying.

WHAT IF THE DISCIPLES HAD NEVER MULTIPLIED?

STEPS TO HEALTHY MULTIPLICATION

Knowing how to multiply will lessen the blow for a small group. There are 10 steps to healthy multiplication highlighted in *Becoming Small Group Leaders* by Keith Madsen and Lyman Coleman. [23] Use these with your G1 group. Remember to model them because the group leaders will do what they have experienced.

STEP 1: Share a vision.

The vision to multiply must be cast from the very first group meeting. God can greatly affect the larger body of Christ if small groups share a desire to bring people into the Kingdom. If the group creates a covenant that envisions multiplication, new groups will happen. An effective leader regularly keeps this goal in front of the group. It's important to divide into new groups every 18-24 months. Make sure you regularly announce the group's intention to multiply.

STEP 2: Build a new leadership team.

As the group grows, develops, and matures, the present leadership team should identify apprentice leaders and facilitators. This is done best in a small-group setting.

- Identify apprentice leaders and facilitators.
- Provide on-the-job training.
- Give future leaders the opportunity to lead your group.
- Introduce the new leadership team to your church.
- Launch the new group.

STEP 3: Determine the type of group to be formed.

Who are you trying to reach? Refer to Section 3, Chapter 13 for a listing of the basic group types.

STEP 4: Conduct a Needs Survey.

Use either a custom survey for your church or download the one included on the Web at *www.SerendipityHouse.com/Community* to determine an area of need or a specific topic for your first study.

STEP 5: Choose a discussion topic or curriculum.

Make sure your choice fits the group type and the maturity level of your group.

STEP 6: Ask someone to serve as host.

Determine when and where the group will meet. Someone must coordinate the following:

- Where the meeting will be held.
- Who will provide babysitters (if necessary).
- Who will teach children (if necessary).
- Who will provide refreshments.

STEP 7: Decide who will go with the new team.

Use the guidance in this chapter to assist you with this step.

⊜ **STEP 8: Begin a countdown.**

An unexpected announcement that the group will be multiplying the next week can kill the hearts of the individual group members and their passion for groups. Let the group know that it will be multiplying well in advance of the change. Eight weeks will allow people time to grieve and accept the idea of multiplication.

⊜ **STEP 9: Celebrate.**

The last group meeting together should be a time to celebrate everything the group has experienced together. The questions below will open a discussion that will lead into a time of celebration.

- What's the most humorous moment you experienced while a part of this group?
- What was the most inspiring moment you witnessed as we shared life together? Why did this moment mean so much to you and to the group?
- How has your life been changed by being a part of this small group?

After this moving discussion, have each group pray for the other as they invite others to join them into compelling community.

⊜ **STEP 10: Keep casting a vision.**

From the very first meeting of each new group, the leaders should repeat Step 1 and begin casting the vision for the group to multiply in 18–24 months.

EMPOWERING YOUR GROUP

Like childbirth, multiplication is painful; but new, life-changing relationships are on the other side of the pain. A strong leader will empower his or her group members to embrace the need for multiplication.

Empowering people isn't difficult. *The Oxford Dictionary* describes empowerment as "to give power or authority to." Small-group leaders must first be empowered by their church body to lead a small congregation, disciple believers, and lead the lost to Jesus. I would suggest that this occur publicly in a church-wide service specifically designed for the empowering and commissioning of these leaders. This will add validity to the role of small-group leader and establish the importance of this work in the minds of the congregation. It will also create momentum for the ministry by giving these leaders credibility as they begin to recruit group members in the days that follow. In turn, small-group leaders need to empower their group members to do the same. The result is a healthy ministry that rapidly and powerfully multiplies.

DESTINATION:COMMUNITY

SECTION FIVE
THE SMALL-GROUP MEETING

WITH APOLOGIES TO WILLIAM SHAKESPEARE ...

To meet or not to meet—that is the question.

Whether 'tis nobler in the mind to suffer the stings and boredom of these ridiculous time-wasters, or to take up our backsides and plant them elsewhere, and by our absence end them.

5 A MATTER OF LIFE AND DEATH

Most of us hate meetings; maybe that's because they are often planned and executed as though the meeting is the event. This is certainly true of the approach utilized by many small-group systems.

Too often people in small groups believe and act like they signed up for a weekly meeting. If this philosophy permeates the leaders and the majority of small-group members in a given group, that small group will crash and burn. Simply having a weekly meeting kills a small group. While the meeting is an essential and primary part of the small-group experience, it cannot be seen as the core encounter of group life. Being a part of a small group requires that members share their lives, and life happens all week long. The small-group meeting is only one small aspect of doing life together. No group can become a redemptive community and experience meaningful levels of Christian growth if they simply meet once a week. Acts 2 tells us that the believers were together "daily" (Acts 2:46).

Most of you will want to use this section of the book as a reference guide that you can return to again and again. Therefore, this section, like the others, is set up so you can easily find information on the topics for which most leaders seek answers. You'll find lists throughout these short chapters so that you can quickly get the information you need. Use these as quick guides to answer specific questions you might be asking yourself, checklists for meeting preparations, and methods for evaluating your group.

26 CHAPTER

MEETING TIPS

ACTIVITIES GUIDE TO BURNING CALORIES

(includes calories consumed per hour)

- Beating around the bush – 75
- Jumping to conclusions – 100
- Climbing the walls – 150
- Throwing your weight around – 300

- Passing the buck – 25
- Swallowing your pride – 50
- Dragging your heels – 100
- Pushing your luck – 250

For the rest of the list, read on …

STRONG MEETINGS

Even though the small-group meeting is only a part of your group life, it is an important time when you gather everyone for a focused time together. So, be sure your meeting is well-planned and well-led. It must be satisfying and enjoyable in order for the group members to want to return. The short chapters that follow will help you to create a meeting experience that group members won't want to miss. A great small-group meeting should include time:

- to affirm, console, encourage, learn, and celebrate
- to reveal and meet member's needs
- to share stories and ask God to heal areas where the enemy is holding us captive
- to discover, discuss, and embrace biblical principles and expectations
- for group members to encourage and to hold one another accountable for living out biblical principles and expectations
- to plan ministry opportunities that the group will carry out together
- to allow the group's apprentice to practice his or her skills
- for a pre-Christian to see God's people connecting with God and with one another
- to worship together
- to pray for one another
- for group members to utilize their spiritual gifts to accomplish together what they couldn't have accomplished alone

CREATE AN EXPERIENCE GROUP MEMBERS WON'T WANT TO MISS!

MEETING TIPS

Here are a few things to keep in mind as you begin to plan for your meetings:

⊜ Every time your group meets, it's composed of a variety of personalities.

In *How to Handle Impossible People, High-Maintenance Relationships*, Les Parrot describes various difficult personality types that you will most likely encounter in your small group. The list includes ...

- The Critic – who constantly complains and gives unwanted advice.
- The Martyr – who is a "victim" wracked with self-pity.
- The Wet Blanket – who is pessimistic and negative.
- The Steamroller – who is blindly insensitive to others.
- The Gossip – who spreads rumors and leaks secrets.
- The Control Freak – who is unable to let go and let be.
- The Backstabber – who is irrepressibly two-faced.
- The Cold Shoulder – who disengages and avoids conflict.

- The Green-Eyed Monster – who seethes with envy.
- The Volcano – who builds steam and then erupts.
- The Sponge – who constantly needs but gives nothing back.
- The Competitor – who keeps score about everything.
- The Workhorse – who always pushes and is never satisfied.
- The Flirt – who exudes innuendoes that border on harassment.
- The Chameleon – who blends in and avoids conflict. [24]

DIVERSITY IS A BIG CHALLENGE

This list is just the tip of the iceberg when it comes to the types of people you'll have in the room each time you meet. Because your group is diverse, don't anticipate the same responses from each attendee and don't expect the small-group members to always agree. This is the challenging part of dealing with people. But it's this same diversity of ideas, life stories, and perspectives that will make your group meetings rich and exhilarating.

BUT DIVERSITY CREATES EXCITEMENT

⊜ **Every time your group meets, your members are facing multiple complex life situations.**
For some reason we think that everybody else has life going well and all figured out. We want grace given to us because we're having a bad day, because we just weren't aware of how we came across to others, or because we just said something stupid. On the other hand, we jump to conclusions, expect near perfection in others, and get angry instead of extending grace to other people.

WE WASTE OUR ENERGIES AND RUIN COMMUNITY

Here's the comprehensive list of scientific data on the activities in which we all tend to engage. It comes from another e-mail that has been forwarded around the globe.

ACTIVITIES GUIDE TO BURNING CALORIES (includes calories consumed per hour)

Beating around the bush – 75	Hitting the nail on the head – 50
Jumping to conclusions – 100	Wading through paperwork – 300
Climbing the walls – 150	Bending over backwards – 75
Swallowing your pride – 50	Jumping on the bandwagon – 200
Passing the buck – 25	Running around in circles – 350
Throwing your weight around – 50-300	Eating crow – 225
Dragging your heels – 100	Tooting your own horn – 25
Pushing your luck – 250	Climbing the ladder of success – 750
Making mountains out of molehills – 500	Pulling out the stops – 75

Adding fuel to the fire – 160

Opening a can of worms – 50

Putting your foot in your mouth – 300

Starting the ball rolling – 90

Going over the edge – 25

Picking up the pieces after a mess– 350

Counting chickens before they hatch – 60

Calling it quits – 20

Obviously, we could spend all of this negative energy in much more constructive, redemptive ways!

EXTEND THE GRACE YOU'D LIKE TO RECEIVE

◉ **Every time your group meets, a variety of underlying factors affect the way people respond.** Varying attitudes, hidden feelings, and unresolved conflicts are bound to affect the way your members respond to the experiences they encounter during the meeting. The mantra of any successful group must be the apostle Peter's instruction to "keep love at full strength." Let's look this in context …

⁷ Now the end of all things is near; therefore, be clear-headed and disciplined for prayer. ⁸ Above all, keep your love for one another at full strength, since love covers a multitude of sins. ⁹ Be hospitable to one another without complaining. ¹⁰ Based on the gift they have received, everyone should use it to serve other, as good managers of the varied grace of God.

1 Peter 4:7-10

KEEP LOVE AT FULL STRENGTH

◉ **Every time your group meets, unresolved issues caused by past experiences may trigger individual group members to respond emotionally to subjects you're discussing.**

◉ **Every time your group meets, God wants to transcend all of the differences mentioned above and touch every person in the group.**

LET GOD HELP YOU TRANSCEND DIFFERENCES

As you can see, your members will carry a lot of baggage with them into group meetings. So will you! Be sensitive to individual emotions, situations, and inner turmoil each time your group gets together. There will be times when you'll ask a group member to aggressively approach a personal issue in order to move toward its resolution. There will be times when, because of the rawness of a situation, you gently allow a group member to reveal painful circumstances in his or her own time.

CHAPTER 27

BEFORE THE MEETING

PREPARING FOR YOUR SMALL-GROUP TIME is more like a quarterback preparing for a big game than like a Bible-study leader studying to present information. It demands that you stay in spiritual shape. You must know what your players are going through, what their standing is with the coach, and what you hope to accomplish in and through them when the group is together. If you prepare well in advance, you can pass them the ball during your meeting and expect them to run with it. In most instances, they will.

PREP BEFORE YOU STEP

For a group meeting to be successful, it's important that the group leader prepare well. Serendipity House Bible studies include leader notes to review before each meeting, but there is much more a group leader must do to be ready for the group meeting, including aspects of his or her personal life that will have nothing to do with the meeting itself. In order for a small-group leader to lead the kind of experience that will draw members back to each meeting, several key things must be in place.

A GREAT GROUP LEADER MUST BE ON THE JOURNEY

Leaders must know the character and heart of God in order to tell small-group members how He wants to work in their lives. We can't take people to places that we've never gone ourselves. Leaders must be on their own redemptive journeys with God if they're going to take others anywhere.

WE CAN'T TAKE PEOPLE PLACES WE'VE NEVER GONE

Listening for God's Voice
When Jesus taught His disciples, He said, *"I am the Vine, you are the branches. When you're joined with me and I with you, the relation intimate and organic, the harvest is sure to be abundant. Separated, you can't produce a thing"* (John 15:5, Message). The only way leaders will impact others' lives is through the supernatural power of Jesus. The most essential responsibility a small-group leader has is to stay closely connected to Jesus on a daily basis. We hear from God primarily through the Bible and prayer, but He also speaks to us as we take our deepest questions to God, open a dialog with our hearts, and stay alert to God's voice revealed in unique ways such as group interaction, nature, media, art, and circumstances.

Cell church guru Joel Comiskey once surveyed 700 small-group leaders. His survey revealed that the success of the small group depended on how much time the group leader spent in daily focused time with God.

Be Willing to Enter into Unfamiliar Places with God
More than anything else, the redemptive journey requires us to trust God. God will lead us down unfamiliar paths to healing, freedom, and growth. We must take one day and one step at a time even as we walk into the shadows with God, allow Him to turn the shadows to light, ease our pain, and lead us into freedom, truth, and the true desires of our hearts. In Isaiah 42:16 God says, *"I will lead the blind by ways they have not known, along unfamiliar paths I will guide them; I will turn the darkness into light before them and make the rough places smooth. These are the things I will do; I will not forsake them"* (NIV).

STAY CLOSELY CONNECTED TO GOD

Praying for Wisdom
There will be many times when members will need wise counsel from their small group leader. James says, *"If any of you lacks wisdom, he should ask God, who gives generously to all without finding fault, and it will be given to him"* (James 1:5, NIV).

Inviting the Holy Spirit to Infuse You and Your Group
Paul the apostle tells us, *"Don't get drunk with wine, which leads to reckless actions, but be filled with the Spirit"* (Ephesians 5:18). In Greek, the words "be filled" refer to the need for a continual infusion of the Spirit's presence and power in your life.

Talking with God About All Your Failures
David wrote, *"I cried out to [God] with my mouth; his praise was on my tongue. If I had cherished sin in my heart, the Lord would not have listened; but God has surely listened and heard my voice in prayer. Praise be to God, who has not rejected my prayer or withheld his love from me!"* (Psalm 66:17-20, NIV).

Getting Kingdom-Focused
Jesus says, *"Steep your life in God-reality, God-initiative, God-provisions. Don't worry about missing out. You'll find all your everyday human concerns will be met"* (Matthew 6:33, Message). When leaders make God's Kingdom their first priority, God will bless their small groups in many ways.

THE FOCUS OF THE MISSION IS THE KINGDOM

Praying for Each Group Member by Name daily
We should follow Jesus' example in praying specifically for individuals in our care: *"Simon, I've prayed for you in particular that you not give in or give out. When you have come through the time of testing, turn to your companions and give them a fresh start"* (Luke 22:32, Message).

FOCUS ON INDIVIDUAL NEEDS

Praying with the Group Apprentice
Pray with the group apprentice for the meeting 15 minutes before it starts. Remember to invite the Holy Spirit to join you and to work in the hearts of each group member. Then greet the attendees together as they show up for the meeting.

A GREAT GROUP LEADER DOES MORE THAN TALK

To lead a group well, a group leader must integrate the upcoming truths from the group's study into his or her own life experience. Someone once asked a group leader how far ahead of the group he needed to be. The leader's response was "One week." A leader needs to be on the journey, but that doesn't at all mean that the leader has arrived.

Small-group leaders don't have to be Bible scholars in order to be models for their group members. However, they do need to personally test biblical principles that they are passing on to group members. When a leader shares how a certain principle has personally impacted his or her life, the group members are encouraged to become *"doers of the word and not hearers only"* (James 1:22).

A GREAT GROUP LEADER CREATES AN EXPERIENCE

You may notice that I purposely didn't use the word "study." A small-group meeting that is powered by the need to complete an agenda designated by a curriculum will leave everyone wanting. A small-group meeting that is motivated by the need to reshape people's hearts will become an experience. Group members seldom remember gatherings in which they went through the motions to complete a study. However, they never forget meetings that evolve into experiences. You want your group members to leave saying, "I can't believe what we experienced tonight!" Because of this, Serendipity House resources are incorporating a greater level of experiential and transformational elements.

Focus on taking people on a journey rather than on completing a session or unit of study. Great small-group studies create an environment where a meeting can easily turn into an "experience." A good launching point is to begin with a four-part agenda. With this model, the meeting time is broken up into four segments that include Breaking the Ice, Discovering the Truth, Embracing the Truth, and Connecting.

⊝ Breaking the Ice
Each meeting should begin with icebreakers questions or activities. Use fun, uplifting questions or interactions designed to warm up the group and help people get to know one another better. One goal for icebreakers is that every group member hear himself speak and that the leader affirms him for sharing. After receiving affirmation, members will be much more apt to speak up later. Breaking the Ice questions should focus on topics that are universal for every person in the group. They might include questions about childhood, teen years, hobbies, and humorous experiences. You can also effectively use movie scenes, video clips, music, or hands-on activities to launch your meeting.

⊝ Discovering the Truth
Discovering the Truth follows the Breaking the Ice time. This is the interactive Bible study portion of the meeting. The goal of this time is for the group to discover biblical truths through open discovery questions that lead to further investigation. The goal is to

lead people into the joy of discovering fresh insights. Everyone should participate in the Discovering the Truth discussions. Even though people have differing levels of biblical knowledge, it's vital that they encourage each other to share what they are observing, thinking, and feeling about the Bible passages.

INTEGRATE TRUTH INTO LIFE

Embracing the Truth

All studies should direct group members to action and life change. The Embracing the Truth section continues the Bible-study time with an emphasis on leading group members to integrate the biblical truths they have discovered into their lives. Embracing the Truth questions should be very practical and application-focused. More personal self-disclosure begins to occur during the latter part of your meeting.

CONNECT WITH GOD, YOUR HEART, AND OTHERS

Connecting

One of the key goals of every good small-group experience is to lead group members to grow closer to one another as they develop a sense of community. The Connecting time provides opportunities for the group to encourage, support, and pray for one another. Be sure to close each of your times together with an opportunity for group members to connect with God, with their own hearts, or with each other.

A workable schedule for a small-group meeting might be ...
- Greet attendees, mingle, and find a seat – 5 minutes
- Breaking the Ice – 10-15 minutes
- Discovering the Truth – 20 minutes
- Embracing the Truth – 15-20 minutes
- Connecting – 10-15 minutes
- Snacks and personal interactions – 30 minutes

GREAT GROUP LEADERS EVALUATE

FOCUS ON SHEPHERDING PEOPLE

Remember that your key focus is shepherding the people in your group, not leading a study. In order for you to be sensitive to special moments, you must be aware of your group members' situations. Prior to each meeting, take a few moments and answer the following questions related to each group member's present situation. This activity will help you to discern if there's a need to veer from the agenda to allow God to minister to a specific group member.

- What's life like at home?
- What's life like at work?
- How are the key relationships with which this group member is involved?
- What desire is not coming to fruition?
- With what tough questions is God forcing this person to wrestle?
- What failure has entered this person's world this week?
- What expectations has God placed on this person that he or she needs to realize and accept?

GREAT GROUP LEADERS GROW APPRENTICES

If an apprentice leader is going to develop and mature, he or she needs to own some substantial responsibility within the group. In order for the apprentice to become a great small-group leader, he or she must have the opportunity to lead some portion of the group meeting. This doesn't necessarily have to happen every week but give the apprentice this chance on a regular basis. Be certain you model what you are asking the apprentice to do. Evaluate his or her work by revealing what was done right and give constructive criticism. Finally, allow the apprentice to try again and again and again until he or she experiences success. It will make a huge difference if you begin small and enable the apprentice to build upon a sequence of smaller successes.

WORK TO REPLICATE YOURSELF

GREAT GROUP LEADERS CREATE THE RIGHT ENVIRONMENT

It's amazing how much the environment in the place you meet affects the group dynamics. Find ways to create a comfortable and relaxing environment before the group members arrive. Here are some ideas …

PEOPLE NEED HELP TO RELAX

- Light a scented candle and play quiet music. Many group members will be rushing in from work. Create a relaxing environment that will calm nerves and settle spirits.
- Set the room temperature between 68 and 70 F°. This will be cool for early arrivals, but as the room fills the temperature will be comfortable for most group members.
- Remove all pets from the meeting area. While some people will tell you they enjoy your pets, those who don't speak up may be allergic or frightened of your animals.
- Light the room enough so people can read but not so much that they're uncomfortable.
- Arrange the seats in a way that is conducive for conversation. A circle is best when possible. Make sure members can look into each other's eyes. Have a seat designated for the group leader. Space the chairs about 18 inches to 4 feet apart to encourage deeper levels of interaction.
- As group members arrive, ask them to silence cell phones, only taking calls from babysitters.

I hope you've caught the message that being a great small-group leader has far less to do with what you do to prepare for a meeting than it does with who you are, your care for the individuals in your group, and the authenticity of your spiritual journey.

**CARE FOR YOUR PEOPLE
GET ON THE JOURNEY
TAKE OTHERS WITH YOU**

28 CHAPTER

DURING THE MEETING

WHAT WOULD HAPPEN if Jesus really did show up at our small-group meetings? Could it really be the way it was when Jesus walked the earth? He preached good news to the poor, bound up the brokenhearted, proclaimed freedom to the captives, and released from darkness those who were spiritually and emotionally enslaved. He also replaced ashes with a crown of beauty and shame with glory (see Isaiah 61:1-3).

If we would welcome Jesus into our meetings and He actually showed up, how could our meetings or our lives ever be the same again?!

REASONABLY FANTASTIC!

Treasure your meeting time. It's the only occasion in the week when your whole group will come together and expect God to do something fantastic. *"Where two or three come together in my name, there am I with them"* (Matthew 18:20, NIV). You will want to make sure that you lead the meeting effectively. If you do, wonderful things will likely occur. In order for you to lead great small-group experiences, it will be important for you to consider the following suggestions:

⊜ BE AN ACTIVE LISTENER.

The Chinese characters that depict the verb "to listen" incorporate the ears, eyes, undivided attention, and heart. We listen from the heart when we value and respect the person speaking. We should feel this way about every member in our small group. Show group members that you're listening by reacting appropriately to what they say. Allow your body language to show you're an active listener. Smile or nod your head in agreement. Laugh if something is funny. Make eye contact with the person speaking. Don't glance at the clock or someone else in the room when a group member is talking to you. Don't shift in your seat as though what is being said is boring you or making you uncomfortable. So that the group members know you're not closing them off, don't cross your arms or legs. Lean forward in your chair to show you're interested in what the person is saying. Most importantly, listen with your heart and your body will follow.

LISTEN WITH YOUR EYES, EARS, AND FULL ATTENTION
MOST OF ALL, LISTEN WITH YOUR HEART

⊜ LIMIT MONOLOG AND FACILITATE DIALOG.

Great small-group facilitators talk less than 10% of the time. If you create an environment where you fill the gaps of silence, the group will quickly learn that they don't need to join you in the conversation.

⊜ STEER THE GROUP TO GREATER LEVELS OF COMMUNICATION.

There are seven basic levels of communication: non-participation, clichés, facts, impressions, opinions, personal sharing, and full disclosure. As the group meets, you'll want to evaluate which of these stages the group is in and ask questions that help people move to the next stage. Be aware that there will be times when most of the group moves forward and one or two lag behind. Help the trailing group members to catch up to the others by wisely asking them questions that move them to greater levels of disclosure. We find the deepest levels of healing and transformation with greater levels of disclosure.

GREATER LEVELS OF DISCLOSURE FOSTER
HEALING AND TRANSFORMATION

⊜ ASK GOOD QUESTIONS.

There are basically two types of questions: closed-ended and open-ended. You will know a closed-ended question because one of three things will happen. The group may quickly give the right answer and force you to immediately move to the next question. They may dig through the lesson searching for the correct fiil-in-the-blank answer or give you a yes or no reply. All three of these responses indicate that the question asked was closed-ended because it didn't lead to further discussion. On the other hand, an open-ended question draws people out into further conversation.

OPEN-ENDED QUESTIONS DRAW PEOPLE INTO FURTHER DISCUSSION

Make sure that you prepare to ask four kinds of questions during your meeting time. Most of these should be open-ended, and only some will be closed.

Observation Questions – Observation questions ask, "What is the Bible telling us?" The answer to this question is found in Scripture. Ask this type of question when you want the group to tell you what they see in the verses you're discussing.

Interpretation Questions – Interpretation questions ask, "What does this verse mean?" These questions can make for lively discussions. During the conversation, it's all right to allow many ideas to float through the air. Just be sure that the truth lands.

JOY OF DISCOVERING FRESH INSIGHTS INTO FURTHER DISCUSSION

Application Questions – Application questions lead group members to decide how they're going to integrate what's been learned into their lives. They've learned what the Bible says by having taken the time to evaluate where they stand in light of this knowledge. Through the application questions, group members consider changing their activities or, more importantly, what they think or believe. It's our deepest held beliefs that drive our behavior. Most application questions are open-ended and lead to a commitment to change.

OUR DEEPEST BELIEFS DRIVE OUR BEHAVIOR

Evaluation Questions – Evaluation questions ask, "How am I doing in this area of my life?" Questions of this nature help the small-group members realize paradigm shifts they need to make or actions they need to take. These are the questions that open the door for self-disclosure and sharing stories with one another.

The power of open-ended questions is giving group members the joy of discovering fresh insights and applications of God's truth.

⊜ MODEL TRANSPARENCY.

"The small group you lead will only be as transparent as you are." The first time I heard this statement, I was flabbergasted. It never occurred to me that I would have to be transparent. Being open about your own life can be very intimidating. We wonder what others will think of us. We're not certain that what we unveil won't get voiced outside of the group. For many of us, we've never been in a home or with friends where transparency was modeled. In fact, you may not know any more about your own parents than a few embarrassing moments they've been willing to share with you. When it comes to becoming transparent, many of us are stepping out onto what feels like dangerous ground.

TAKE THE RISK TO LEAD THE WAY DON'T DIVE IN ALL AT ONCE

Being transparent with your small group is a worthwhile risk. But don't dive in all at once. Slowly move your group toward a deeper level of communication one step at a time. As the group leader, you'll be the one to put your foot in the water first to check out the temperature. See how people respond and then move accordingly. Here are a few suggestions for modeling transparency for your group members:

1. **Start by telling your story.** Over time, tell all of your story, including the hard times that transformed your life. Explain how God was at work in those times. You will feel like you're telling more about God than you are about yourself.

2. **When appropriate, tell the group about a present struggle that's causing you inner turmoil.** A work situation or non-family situation may be less intimidating to share initially.

3. **Share temptations you've faced in the last week.** Every person in the group is tempted. Be careful to reveal temptations that are gender safe. For instance, you wouldn't want to talk about a temptation to go back to pornographic Web sites in mixed company.

4. **Confess your failures, struggles, and sin.** Now we've hit the mound of messy and memorable conversation. When you reveal sin to the group, be certain to choose the audience wisely. In most instances, it's best to subgroup into male and female groupings if group members are to be open about sins with which they struggle.

As you can see, the group leader needs to be intentionally integrated into every moment of the group experience and into the lives of each individual in attendance. As you model connection, others will join you by connecting with one another. Your attention to the suggestions noted in this Section 5 will create a dynamic that will open the doors of conversation and lead to the group connection for which you're longing.

MOVE TOWARD THE CONNECTION FOR WHICH YOU LONG

29 CHAPTER

AFTER THE MEETING

WELCOME to what may be the shortest chapter in any small-groups book ever written!

EVALUATION QUESTIONS

As a group leader, I have found that answering a few probing questions after each meeting helps me know what I need to do between meetings. I hope the list below will serve you just as well.

1. **Is there someone for whom I need to pray?**

2. **Is there someone who needs counsel?**

3. **Is there someone to encourage?**

4. **Is there someone to hold accountable?**

5. **Is there something to celebrate with someone?**

6. **Is there something to learn?**

7. **Is there a need to be met?**

8. **Is there a leadership call to make?**

9. **Is there a conflict to be resolved?**

10. **What is God up to?**

WHAT IS GOD UP TO?

30 CHAPTER

BETWEEN MEETINGS

AUTHENTIC COMMUNITY is created between meetings. Most groups meet for 1.5 hours per week. That means there are another 166.5 hours in the week when group members aren't connected to the rest of the group. As the leader, you need to make sure you stay connected to your group all week long.

THE REST OF THE STORY ...

Authentic community is created between meetings because it's in doing life together that relationships are developed and deepened. There are a number of things you can do to develop deeper connections between meetings. Outside of the group meeting, make sure that you make the following connections:

COMMUNITY IS CREATED BETWEEN MEETINGS

⊜ Connect with group members.
This doesn't have to involve a long phone conversation or personal visit to someone's home. An e-mail may suffice. There are specific situations that elicit different responses. The list below may be helpful to you as the group leader.

- To pass information – e-mail is appropriate.
- To congratulate someone on a special occasion – a card will do.
- To celebrate a life achievement – dinner or a party with the group would be super.
- To comfort someone in a time of crisis – a visit to the home is best.

⊜ Get group members together just for fun.
Spending time together during the week doesn't have to happen often, but it should happen on a monthly basis. If you want to connect more deeply with a group member, meet with him or her individually (don't meet alone with a member of the opposite sex, especially if you're married) and do something together that's unrelated to the group. If you see someone really struggling to fit in with the entire group, get him or her to connect with a few group members for a night of relaxation. It may be just the thing to make the member feel more at home with the group.

GET TOGETHER JUST FOR FUN
DO LIFE TOGETHER

MEET ONE-ON-ONE TOO

⊜ Encourage group members to connect.
Take the opportunity regularly to encourage connection between group members outside of meetings. Be aware of people who are being left out or opting out; take steps when needed to provide special attention to integrating these group members.

Make sure that the needs of the group are met.

Any time you hear that a group member has a need, respond immediately. Ask other group members to help you in giving care, making home improvements, or helping with the heating bill.

Meet regularly with the leadership team.

You'll need to meet with the small-group leadership team periodically to share impressions, brainstorm ideas, and strategize future group experiences.

Mentor the group's apprentice.

The group apprentice needs to have the opportunity to be with you when you carry out the responsibilities of a group leader. When possible, invite this person to go with you when you minister to the people in your group. Afterwards, debrief with the apprentice and explain why you did what you did. Next time, ask the apprentice to do what you previously modeled. Evaluate the apprentice's work and redirect him or her as necessary.

WORK TOGETHER WITH YOUR LEADERS

Pray for and with the group members.

Prayer is the most important responsibility you have as a small-group leader. Pray every day for each of your group members individually. Pray for their specific life situations and for the growth you long to see take place in their lives. Ask them what you can pray for on their behalf and then pray for them on a daily basis. Be sure to let them know you're upholding them in prayer.

BUY SOME KNEEPADS HIT THE FLOOR

Celebrate with group members when appropriate.

When group members experience significant life breakthroughs, take the time to call and congratulate them. This gesture will speak volumes about your interest in their lives. On special occasions a party may be appropriate.

IT ALL BOILS DOWN TO A FEW KEY WORDS ...

FRIENDSHIP ... LEADERSHIP ... COMMUNITY ... JOURNEY ...

TRANSFORMATION ... REDEMPTION ... MISSION ... ADVENTURE ...

and LARGER STORY

DESTINATION:COMMUNITY

SECTION SIX
YOUTH SMALL GROUPS by JOSH HOWERTON

YOUTH MINISTRY IS INVIGORATING and discouraging at the same time. One minute you're on top of the world wondering if you'll convert your city by the end of the semester, and the next minute you receive one sour comment from a parent and begin to question if you were even called to work with youth in the first place.

6 RESCUE MISSION TO A LOST BUT UNBELIEVABLY INSIGHTFUL GENERATION

If you're in youth ministry, you've probably been discouraged (if not today, maybe yesterday or last month). I've been there.

I once had a high-school student who hadn't yet crossed the line to faith say something profound to me. I was trying to share the gospel with a guy named Davyd one night in the middle of a discouraging period in my life, and I asked him why he was so turned off by anybody from our ministry who tried to love him. He responded, "Everybody around here always tries to act like they're so happy. If they'll lie about that, why should I believe 'em when they say they care about me?" Great question … great enough for me to remember it more than a year later.

One reason why it's so easy to get discouraged working with today's youth is because of the general aura that surrounds them. The reigning assumption of the vast majority of students in the youth culture is skepticism—the only universally accepted standard our students have right now. So, when student "x" walks into church for the first time and sees everyone wearing clothes they don't wear anywhere else, saying words they don't say anywhere else (like "benediction" and, my personal favorite, "vestibule"), using voice intonations that they don't use anywhere else (i.e. "preaching voices"), and smiling as if they've never had a bad day, student "x" doesn't just *think* what he's seeing is fake, he **knows** what he's seeing is fake.

The good news is that there's hope. In the midst of skepticism, authenticity interrupts. The vehicle for this interruption in youth ministry is small groups.

CHAPTER 31

ADVANTAGES OF SMALL GROUPS IN STUDENT MINISTRY

WHAT DO ALL THESE popular, student phenomena have in common?

- www.MySpace.com
- Hanging out at the coffee shops
- www.FaceBook.com
- Drinking or drug buddies
- Gangs
- Sports teams or other clubs
- www.YouTube.com

They ALL provide connection, belonging, purpose, and community!

EFFECTS OF POSTMODERNISM

I love what Erwin McManus, pastor of Mosaic Church in Los Angeles, said recently, "If you're using the word 'postmodern,' you're not." Classical postmodernism, the predominant cultural philosophy coming out of the '90s, has left its residue in the minds of contemporary thinkers. One key tenet was "no verbal communication can convey objective truth" because of differing word connotations in various cultures. The hearer determined what "truth" any communication held. This attitude left the postmodern world reeling for a source of Truth, so it turned to experience. On the positive side, postmodernism pointed out two things student ministries must understand: the persuasiveness of experience and the overwhelming influence of culture.

EXPERIENCE IS PERSUASIVE & CULTURE IS INFLUENTIAL

ENTER SMALL GROUPS ...

The beauty of small groups for student ministry is the ability to meet students in their culture and impact them in intimate environments where they can experience the blazing reality of hearts transformed by God's Spirit. Christian philosopher William Lane Craig noted in his essay "Five Views on Apologetics" that he didn't become a Christian because of a philosophic argument. He did so because his "Christian friends were living on a different plane of reality." This reminds me of Paul's words to the Corinthians: *"I came to you in weakness and fear, and with much trembling. My message and my preaching were not with wise and persuasive words, but with a demonstration of the Spirit's power, so that your faith might not rest on men's wisdom, but on God's power"* (1 Corinthians 2:3-5 NIV). Paul didn't simply try to argue them into faith. His ministry demonstrated the Truth

HELP THEM EXPERIENCE THE BLAZING REALITY OF HEARTS TRANSFORMED BY GOD

CLONING YOURSELF

A few weeks ago I experienced one of the most humbling and awe-inspiring weeks of ministry. I was supposed to teach about prayer during our large-group worship time, but 30 minutes before our first service I felt God leading me to pray with my students instead. We prayed, and God poured out His Spirit on us in response. Afterwards, three students put their trust in Jesus for salvation and two others revealed some very serious issues with which they were dealing. Those kinds of moments solidify for me that I couldn't possibly do anything but pastor. They also leave me realizing that I have five significant follow-up meetings to cram into next week's schedule. Thankfully, I can lean on our Life Groups.

Small groups can save you unspeakable amounts of time as a youth pastor. More than any other group, teens require individual counsel on issues in their lives. Essentially, your student ministry has as many ministers as there are small-group leaders. In fact, small groups make fulfilling Paul's command to "pay careful attention to yourselves and to all the flock" possible (Acts 20:28). One of the best books a youth minister can pick up for this and other ministry topics is Richard Baxter's *Reformed Pastor*, but I'll warn you—it's old.

**PAY CAREFUL ATTENTION TO THE FLOCK
EVERY GROUP LEADER IS A YOUTH MINISTER**

I don't believe you can really pastor more than 12-15 people and pay careful attention to their individual spiritual lives. Small groups can give students this careful attention.

FLEXING WITH STUDENTS' TIME CRUNCH

They go to school, attend extra-curricular activities at least a two hours a day, work part-time jobs, date, do some chores around the house, and plow through piles of homework. Add in spending time with family and the constant pressure from friends wanting to hang out and you have the stress-inducing schedule of the average student. That's without adding God or church into the mix. The scheduling versatility that small groups provide is sometimes a student's only hope to become deeply connected with other believers.

MEETING STUDENTS' DESPERATE NEED FOR FAMILY

I recently spent the best $400 I've ever spent in student ministry. During the summer, our ministry usually slows down because of family vacations and various camps. During this time, we have "Family Nights" where groups of students meet at a parent's house and hang out together. They play volleyball, grill hotdogs, and basically do family reunion types of activities. I use that rare time when the students are in a more intimate environment and spend eight weeks teaching about the nature and responsibility of biblical community. This summer, I dropped $400 on red wristbands that simply said "Family by Blood." I wanted these wristbands to be a constant reminder that every Christian is a literal brother or sister of every other believer because of the common blood of Jesus that covers us all. Pandemonium ensued! You would've thought we were giving out gold Rolex® watches.

We're blessed with a fairly large student ministry, yet I can count on my fingers and toes the number of students with two married parents who are both involved in church. That's a gaping hole in our students' lives! The wristband stampede didn't happen because the wristbands were cool. You can get them for fifty cents out of a gumball machine. It happened because real Christian community meets a desperate need for family that God put into our hearts. While there's absolutely no substitute for a godly family, small groups act as one for students who, for the most part, are lacking what they need at home.

MAKING A WAY TO STAY

Amazingly, data from a 2004 study released by the Higher Education Research Institute at UCLA shows that 71% of students who graduate from high school abandon participation in church.

As youth ministers, we're preparing students to "graduate into their faith." However, a large number of student ministries are event-based, always looking for the next event that will get students to church. A gospel presentation or biblical teaching is slipped in at the end of the event. The problem with an event-based ministry approach is that when the students are no longer involved in that type of ministry (i.e. any ministry besides youth or children's ministry), they'll be done with church. On the other hand, when students are involved in a ministry that encourages them to accept Christ's call to pursue His Kingdom before anything else, they find a place to belong and tend not to jump ship—because it's their ship. They feel a sense of ownership in the ministry.

THEY DON'T JUMP SHIP ... IT'S THEIR SHIP

We can't have 16-year-olds leading student ministries, but we can involve them in significant ways in the lives of other students and in ministry. They can be Robin to Batman. Small groups are the best way to implement this type of development and mentoring.

RAISING UP STUDENT LEADERS

About a year ago, I taught a series for our student ministry called "Mythbusters" in which I examined some of the commonly held spiritual myths that people believe about Christianity. One week, I addressed the Ashton Kutcher-inspired myth that "Jesus is my Homeboy" and preached from a passage in Revelation where John sees Jesus glorified. God's Spirit anointed the teaching that night, and a lot of students left profoundly impacted by the awesome Savior they worship. I heard stories of students throwing away their "Jesus is my Homeboy" t-shirts and buying David Nasser's "Jesus is not my Homeboy. He is God" t-shirts at a conference. I haven't seen one of the old, trite shirts since. In fact, students in the schools in our area have pretty much abandoned that axiom.

What happened? Our students impacted their culture and shaped it, even if only in a small way. I didn't. In fact, I can't. For that reason, I think the best preliminary step to establishing student small groups is discipling a handful of student leaders so that they're equipped to become catalysts and shape the culture of their future small groups. The great thing about small groups is that more students have the opportunity and encouragement to step up into active leadership roles within each group.

32 CHAPTER

ON YOUR MARK ...
GET SET ... GO!

THE SUMMER AFTER I got engaged to my wife, Jana, I was on staff at a youth camp with a guy she had previously dated. My first day on the campground, I parked my car, unloaded my stuff, and sat down next to the first guy I saw. He was a returning staffer, so, after our introductions, he told me the staffers' names that he knew. Eventually, he came to "the guy," and, after telling me "his" name, he said, "I hear there's some jerk on staff this year that's engaged to his ex-girlfriend." There's nothing like a bad introduction to ruin a relationship before it even starts!

To have a good start with your small groups, be sure to consider creating a vision, recruiting leaders, and executing a successful kickoff.

VISION OR IDIOTIC GENIUS?

Start popping off to a few parents or volunteers about starting a student small-group ministry and you're going to get a bombarded with questions. *Why? What are small groups? When will they meet? Who will lead them? Do I need to accompany Jimmy to his group?* And my personal favorite: *Don't they already do that in Sunday School?*

The best way to sink a great youth ministry idea before it starts is to tell parents (who desperately care about their children) and youth volunteers (who sacrifice extraordinary amounts of time) that you're launching a new ministry without being able to field any pertinent questions they have about it! It's idiotic genius, and it fails every time.

There's no such thing as a cookie-cutter approach to launching a youth small-group ministry because your students, parents, community, facilities, volunteers, church leadership, youth minister, and local masseuse (Are you paying attention or just skimming?) are different than every other church that exists. Here's some advice from the school of hard knocks. Do your homework so you're able to answer the following questions:

NO SUCH THING AS COOKIE-CUTTER APPROACH

- Why small groups?
- How will these groups help our church to better shepherd students?
- Can our available volunteer personnel accomplish the goals we have for small groups? What additional people resources are required?
- What will group meetings look like?
- When, where, and for how long are they going to be held?
- What will we do when groups need to multiply?
- How will we filter new students into groups?
- Will groups be closed or open?

THE ANSWERS TO ALL OF THESE QUESTIONS DEPEND ON YOUR PERSONAL VISION.

The week before I assumed the student ministry position at my church, I took a whole day to pray and study Scripture to solidify a vision in my mind of what God wanted for a vibrant, Spirit-led student ministry. This was the summary result for us at least for now:

My vision for Student Ministry is for Life Groups (the name of our student ministry's small groups) to meet during the week in a large home. During this time, students will celebrate progress on the journey and worship together, then break off into clusters of four to five for relational discipleship and Bible study. "Discipleship" will no longer be a an empty word that students use for hangout time with a "church person," but it will be a time in which students get real, hold each other accountable for sin, and raise the bar in a God-honoring effort to "live the Bible" and the adventure God has for each of them. Lost students will hear about the real, tried, and deep relationships that Christian students have with each other in these groups, and they will want the same thing for themselves. These groups will infect back decks, porches, hot tubs, kitchens, living rooms, fast food restaurants, and pool halls. Places that have previously been filled with sin and spiritual apathy will be awakened to praise, Bible reading, and vibrant, authentic, Christ-like relationships.

A COMPLETE VISION—Don't enter your first small-group ministry conversation without one. You'll look like you're planning to fly a commercial airliner with your eyes closed, and the passengers will find an alternate flight.

RECRUITING GROUP LEADERS

DON'T FALL FOR THE STEREOTYPE

Working in and preaching at student camps have given me an opportunity to observe a lot of youth ministers. For some inexplicable reason, the general consensus among many churches is that a good youth minister is a Hollister-wearing, chic haircutted, iPod® toting, quick-witted, 22-year-old that read C.S. Lewis in high school and has an outgoing personality. Unfortunately, a lot of youth ministers have the same picture in mind when they recruit student ministry volunteers. I've made this mistake and have seen the consequences.

The number one principle in small-group leader recruitment is knowing WHO to ask. Your students can sense a poser like a pickle on their 99¢ double cheeseburger.

One of the best Life Group leaders in our student ministry is "Mr. Birke," a 50-year-old grocery employee with a gut, a t-shirt tucked into his black jeans, and a cross necklace that hangs on a leather strap down to his belly button. And he's not just trying to be different either; that's just who he is. He's also one of the most soft-spoken guys I've ever met. Our hotshot girls' Life Group leaders are all moms who love a good sale anywhere. None of these leaders fit my early stereotypical model, but you'd get the impression from the students that Mr. Birke invented the mp3 player and that the moms personally engineered the first chocolate chip cookie.

Here are some things to look for in a good youth small-group leader ...

◔ **They are real about their faith. (This is the highest priority.)**
If you choose a woman more committed to "religion" and "Southern hospitality" than knowing God and joining in His mission, you're adding to the suspicion that it's all a religious facade for the can't-hack-its in life. Look for people willing to go against the grain for God.

◔ **They relate well to students one-on-one.**
Students make a lot of people really nervous. Weed those people out by watching for candidates who talk one-on-one with students. You don't want somebody that's still trying to fit into the "hip" youth culture. You're looking for spiritual mentors who are on the journey with God.

⊜ **They are responsible and consistent.**

Students are going to miss meetings because the high school team is just one win away from regionals or because somebody ruptured a spleen playing a modified version of "Risk." If a group leader is willing to compromise the group consistency because of outside scheduling conflicts after a meeting time has already been established, students will follow the example.

⊜ **They care about relationships.**

When I sent out our students' Life Group assignments this year, a funny thing happened. Every parent of a student in Ricky Burnette's Life Group from last year called me to request that their son stay in his group. Here's the interesting thing: Ricky isn't even the leader of the group; he's an assistant leader that hardly, if ever, leads. You see, Ricky collects people. Some people collect baseball cards, or stamps, or even floral-patterned neckties. Ricky collects relationships, and he treats them like they're rare and priceless. For example, last year one of Ricky's Life Group members moved five hours away. A normal person signs a card and says, "Bye." Ricky and his Life Group found a way for the guy to stay at their houses for the next month, and then Ricky drove five hours to help him move his stuff and get settled in. Every one of the students in that group got to experience Jesus' heart through Ricky Burnette.

LOOK FOR SPIRITUAL MENTORS ON THE JOURNEY

RICKY COLLECTS PEOPLE

It's important to look for these top four essential qualities in your small-group leaders. Although there are some tendencies you should avoid:

• **People who struggle with negativism or gossip.** The last thing you need is a leader who starts small group every week complaining about the group's disorganization or lack of personal hygiene. You also want to avoid leaders who like to discuss other people.

• **People focused on a theological agenda.** If you've got a leader in mind who's a card-carrying, t-shirt wearing, pre-trib, post-mil, covenant theology-or-die warrior, cross him or her off your list. Don't eliminate this person because of theology, but because he or she cares more about a position than about people and their journeys. The last thing you need is a group of students equating authentic faith with zeal for an ideology.

• **People who struggle with egocentricism.** You're trying to disciple students to become Christians, not Joshians, Jennians, or Rickians. If you ever have a group talking more about how cool their leader is than about the spiritual journey they're experiencing, you may have trouble. Ego always jumps at the opportunity that a youth small group affords —the opportunity to feel young and cool by gathering a bunch of personal disciples.

A final note about leadership recruitment: you're going to have to personally invite the people who will make the best small-group leaders to get involved in your ministry. Good leaders are already involved somewhere, and they aren't going to respond to a blanket request for volunteers at the service on Sunday morning. My conversation with a potentially great small-group leader goes something like this: *"Tony, we're getting ready to launch our Life Groups this semester, and you popped into my head as soon as we started brainstorming names of great leaders. The students love to hang out with you, and you've got incredible life experience. Would you consider leading a group this year?"* Take my advice and memorize that last *"Would you consider"* phrase like it's John 3:16. It makes your request clear without causing people to have a knee-jerk negative reaction to your appeal.

A SUCCESSFUL ANNUAL KICKOFF

Bad introductions can ruin potential relationships, which are exactly what we're praying to develop between small-group leaders and their students. The most important thing you can do to ensure that your students connect to their small group is to host a well-planned small-group kickoff. Think through every moment of the kickoff from the setting to the introductions and try to create the most relationally fertile environment possible. Here are a few suggestions to make your small-group kickoff a success.

- **Try to create anticipation with a draft-day mentality by announcing to students a month in advance that they'll be getting a call from their small-group coaches.**

- **Before the kickoff party, send parents of the students in each group a letter that includes personal biographies of the small-group leaders.** Explain why you chose them to lead and describe how they've demonstrated spiritual maturity. A lot of parents might be wary about entrusting their child's spiritual growth to somebody they don't know. Your stamp of approval and explanation will go a long way with parent.

- **Plan a fun, low-pressure kickoff party for your leaders so that they don't have the added pressure of having to "carry the evening."** This year when our leaders called the students to tell them whose group they were in, they got pizza preferences from every student, and we had a group-selected pizza order on the table as soon as the first students arrived on kickoff night. I followed this with a DVD presentation in which I quickly explained the purposes of our small groups.

- **After the kickoff presentation, encourage your leaders to briefly share their faith journeys with the students.** Students need to know right away that they're being led by someone who's a real person with real struggles and real experience with God.

○ **Provide a small-group covenant for each member.** Students can take it home, read it, sign it, and bring it back to their first meeting. Signatures indicate that they're willing to commit to the group. I've been in both types of groups—adult and student—so I think I can say with complete accuracy that the group covenant is about 56 times more important in a youth small group than in an adult group ... maybe 57 times.

○ **End your kickoff party by doing something fun.** At the end of our kickoff party this year, the students went on a scavenger hunt, taking pictures with disposable cameras. The whole night cost $25 per group, and it was a blast!

A letter was waiting for me in my office the morning after our kickoff night this year. It was from a new group leader, and it confirmed my hopes:

Dear Josh and Jana,

I wanted to thank you for all the work you put into the kickoff event last night.

I love my Life Group! LOVE THEM! They are precious, precious girls, and I enjoyed meeting each and every one of them. Last night when I brought them home, we pulled into my driveway and my family came out to meet the girls. I can't tell you the feeling I had. It felt right. Like I was designed for this purpose. And I was. We all are. We all should be pouring ourselves into others!

We had a lot of fun last night (even though I'm probably too old for late nights like that!). The girls were great sports! When they first came in, most of them didn't even know each other. They just began introducing themselves to one another and talking like they'd been friends for years. They bonded immediately and were so accepting of each other.

I can't wait to dig into the Word and the details of their lives! I'm excited about discipling and learning and teaching and growing and living with them. I feel honored that God is letting me have a Life Group. I loved having them in my home, and I loved having them meet my family because they're now a part of my family.

Although I'm exhausted and feel half-dead, it was worth every minute! Thanks guys. I know it was extremely hard work on your part. Your work paid off and will continue to do so for the rest of their lives (and mine)!

Love you both, Melanie

It's always easier to succeed if you can build on a great beginning. Remember, the goal of your kickoff is to set up your students and their group leaders for relational success.

33 CHAPTER

HANDLING THE WILD ANIMAL

THE YOUTH SMALL-GROUP MEETING is a different animal (and animal is not a misnomer—"rabid marsupial" would probably fit the bill) than any other aspect of ministry. If done well, it's the most powerful tool we have for making lifelong disciples. The problem is that youth small groups are often done poorly.

Do you always have a great day? I don't. Did Jesus always have a great day? I remember times of anger, crying, and even despair in His life. Why do people on the outside think we always have a great day? Because we all struggle with the temptation to cover up.

BE REAL

The number one ingredient that's essential for successful youth small groups is authenticity. In fact, if you have every other essential ingredient in a group meeting but you miss authenticity, it will still fail. Here's a few of the best ways I've found for student group leaders to be authentic:

- Start a meeting by telling your group if you're having a bad day and why.
- Confess appropriate sin to the group and ask for prayer.
- Never show shock or disappointment when someone in your small group confesses past sin. At times that's what students want you to do so they can get attention or have a reason to push you away. They may also be genuinely asking for help.
- Get to know each other by making top ten lists such as "things I like" and "things I hate" because, let's face it, sharing our most embarrassing moments is getting old.
- Tell your faith story without editing out the bad parts of your life. Use wisdom and caution in what or how much detail you share. Don't make light of sin or exaggerate it for the purpose of humor or shock. Just tell your real story.

A few semesters ago our student ministry started reaching out to some of the alternative, gothic students around our area. Christ's healing power is exactly what these hurting students need, and they were slowly finding it. Even today it still takes a long time for us to reach this group. I asked a student who'd come to follow Christ from that background to describe some of the barriers that exist between this group of students and our faith community. Her response was a lot like Davyd's highlighted in the Section 6 introduction. She said, "They hate how Christians always have to have a great day."

THEY HATE HOW CHRISTIANS ALWAYS HAVE TO HAVE A GREAT DAY
FRIENDS OR AN ASSIGNMENT?

FOCUS ON CARING

The second essential ingredient builds on the first—love. Once a student knows you're real, he or she needs to know you really care. If a group leader isn't willing to put down the small-group game plan and listen when a student is hurting, all the students will know that the leader cares more about an agenda than about them. If a leader isn't willing to hang out with them outside of the small-group setting, they'll know that the small group is a mere assignment to the leader.

When I was in middle school, my small-group leader's name was Mike Wilson. Whenever I'm asked who the most influential people on my life as a Christian have been, Mike always tops the list. Mike wasn't cool. He was 35, had a boring job, and no fashion sense. The last year I was in his small group, Mike told us he was getting married (we didn't even know he had a girlfriend). He sent every guy in the group a personal invitation to his wedding, and he sat with us at the reception. From then on, it didn't matter if Mike hit the "cool" mark; we just wanted to be like him because he won our hearts. Before students are going to let you change their lives, they have to know you genuinely care.

TRAIN AS YOU DO LIFE TOGETHER

Recently I had a conversation with a discouraged small-group leader. It seems the girls in her Life Group tune out whatever she says during meetings. Her frustration peaked when she received a call from one of her girls telling her she wouldn't be able to make it to the group meeting "because my mom and I are setting up Halloween decorations." Ouch! Normally in a situation like this one, I might get worried that I had misjudged a person's giftedness or capacity to lead a small group. However, this lady is one of our very best leaders whose Sunday School group connected with her deeply and grew consistently. Now she was saying, "Every time I start teaching, they just want to talk. I end up spending the whole time telling them to pay attention."

Her statement highlighted that this small group was in "red-flag city." It also reveals that I had failed to cast a clear vision for what small-group meetings should look like, and this leader is paying the price.

Another key ingredient for youth small groups is living out God's training plan from Deuteronomy 6:6-7, *"These words that I am giving you today are to be in your heart. Repeat them to your children. Talk about them when you sit in your house and when you walk along the road, when you lie down and when you get up."* The reason our small-group leader was discouraged was that she was "teaching" only with words instead of sharing more naturally as a part of doing life together. Our students need biblical teaching, and there is a time for systematic instruction, but small groups are about creating a community where truth is lived out rather than "taught." I've found that good small-group "teaching" feels like a continuation in the conversation that began when the first student walked in the door.

TRUTH IS LIVED OUT

The philosophic and cultural whirlwind in which students are being raised has left the majority of them with a profound and desperate thirst for something true. Socrates is famous for holding Plato under water until he was almost unconscious and telling him, "When you thirst for truth like you do air, you'll find it." Our students have been under water for however long they've been alive without Christ or the fullness of life and freedom He brings; they're ready for the truth. And as powerful as authentic, loving community in a small group can be, it will never change someone's life in an eternal way ... unless you point him or her to Jesus and a deep personal connection with Him.

YOU CREATE CATALYSTS

I noted earlier that discipling a group of student leaders may be the best way to ensure the success of your small groups. Students tend to have an underlying distrust of adults because their lives and cultures are so different. Avoid picking at the differences such as piercings, music style, dirty jeans, disheveled hair, or his or her latest electronic gadget. Even if you relate well to the students, without a catalyst, it can sometimes take months for an adult group leader to establish trust with students. With a catalyst, it might take only weeks.

Assigning older student leaders (juniors and seniors) to younger groups yields a host of benefits within your small-group ministry.

- It establishes the expectation that students in the youth ministry will serve.
- It intentionally sets up positive peer role models for other students to emulate.
- It alleviates stress on new small-group leaders.
- It breaks down the age wall as an older student sets a relational tone with the leader.
- It disciples future church leaders.

GOOD STUDENT LEADERS WILL BE AMAZING CATALYSTS

For those reasons, I strive to include student leaders working alongside adult leaders who ultimately lead the small groups. Choosing the correct student leaders and pairing them with the appropriate adult leaders is tough. It requires a lot of prayer and personal judgment guided by biblical wisdom. Here's what I look for in my student leaders …

- Students who have been caught serving when it isn't required of them
- Students who have a reputation for standing for a biblical principle when nobody else will
- Students who exhibit a growing love for God and Scripture
- Students who are loving and encouraging toward people they don't know

When it comes time for groups to start meeting, be sure you've communicated the boundaries of the student leaders' authority. In fact, start by not giving them much. Ask them to pray to open the group time or to call to remind students about the meeting. Increase a student leader's involvement as he or she is ready to step up. The most important thing student leaders can do is set the tone for how to respond to the adults' leadership. My wife Jana personally disciples her student leader, Megan, and asks her to come 30 minutes before their group time to go over what they'll discuss. That way Megan is already prepared to break the ice when a question is posed for group response. In fact, a good student leader will be the catalyst for all of the essentials in a youth small group.

34 CHAPTER

FINAL WORDS

MATH ISN'T MY SPECIALTY but the feeling behind this forwarded e-mail sure hits home for many of us.

I've been blaming it on age, poor blood, lack of vitamins, air pollution, saccharin, obesity, dieting, and other maladies that make you wonder if life really is worth living. But I found out it ain't any of those reasons. I'm tired because I'm overworked.

1. *The population of this country is 4 million.*
2. *1 million are retired.*
3. *That leaves 3 million to do the work.*
4. *There are 1 million in school and college.*
5. *That leaves 2 million to do the work.*
6. *250,000 are unemployed and the government employs 750,000.*
7. *That leaves 1 million to do the work.*
8. *200,000 are in the Armed Forces, leaving 800,000 to do the work.*
9. *200,000 are employed by the county council leaving 600,000 to do the work.*
10. *There are 420,000 people in the hospital and 179,998 in prison.*
11. *That leaves 2 people to do the work:* **You and me.**

And you're just sitting around reading this. No wonder I'm so tired!

SUGGESTIONS FOR SENIOR PASTORS

If you're a pastor and you've read this section with your youth minister in mind, you might want to consider not telling him or her at the next staff meeting "You need to start small groups." If you do, this is what he might hear: "what you're doing right now isn't good enough." As you know, the responsibility and pressure that accompany student ministry is so great. Think about the unprecedented cultural chasm that separates parents and teenagers today. Cultural analysts tell us that there hasn't been a philosophic reformation the likes of what is occurring today since the Renaissance. In a given week, a youth minister is expected to be a crisis counselor, spiritual mentor, older brother, event coordinator, babysitter, theologian, role model, family counselor, and personal parental assistant. If incorporating small groups is a direction you'd like to see for the student ministry at your church, be careful not to make it seem like an extra addition to your youth pastor's job description. It will help to ask your youth pastor to meet with you once a week so that the two of you can discuss a chapter of this book together. You have no idea how much your time will mean to him or her.

THOUGHTS FOR YOUTH MINISTERS

Now, if you're a youth minister and you've read this book wishing that your pastor catch the vision for this effective ministry, discuss this with your senior pastor and work as a team. Dividing Christ's church is one of Satan's most common ploys for destroying it. A youth minister can be the most unifying position on a church staff if he's willing to support his pastor unapologetically and behind closed doors with the youth group. Here's a little secret: A pastor who realizes you've got his back with the students and parents will let you do almost anything. Shhh!

A FINAL ENCOURAGEMENT

If you're discouraged because small-group ministry sounds like too big a task, please take heart. God will give you the resources you need to follow the direction He sets for you. Walk with God at His pace. Take one step at a time. AND ENJOY THE RIDE!

SMALL-GROUP RESOURCES FROM SERENDIPITY

SERENDIPITY BIBLICAL STUDIES:

Foundations Series—Takes groups through the process of asking foundational questions to experience a deeper understanding of who God is and who we are.

Understanding the Savior Series—Discuss, comprehend, and perhaps even debate the incredible life, times, and teaching of the Son of God to deepen and transform your life.

Message of Paul Series—Through the letters of Paul, learn to face the challenges of life with the same passion and determination as this revolutionary man of radical faith.

Words of Faith Series—Explores vital dimensions of faith through the study of the themes and truths found in the General Epistles in the New Testament.

MORE Series—An fresh approach to in-depth Bible-study that views Scripture through the lens of the larger story to give you a deeper experience of God and life.

Life Connections® Series—With a wide variety of topics, Life Connections is all you need for great Sunday School, large-group Bible Study, or Adult Bible Fellowship.

SERENDIPITY LIVING LIFE STUDIES:

Home...Works Series—Best-selling marriage and family series by pastor Tommy Nelson helps turn messy marriages into good ones and good marriages into GREAT ones.

God & the Arts Series—Gain fresh spiritual insights as this unique series takes you on a journey through Hollywood blockbusters and music that re-tell the Great Epic story.

Picking Up the Pieces Series—Honest, experiential Bible studies written by leading therapists help you in the journey to recover your heart! Experience the power of healing.

For these and other resources, visit www.SerendipityHouse.com.

DESTINATION:COMMUNITY

CANVAS Series—Using the power of story and art through DVDs and an Experience Guide, this series brings a new multi-media dimension to Bible study.

Life Connections Series—With a wide variety of topics Life Connections is all you need for great Sunday School, large-group Bible Study, or Adult Bible Fellowship.

Fellowship Church Series—Fellowship Church in Dallas/Ft. Worth is a leader in providing culturally relevant, practical Bible studies for a new generation.

Men of Purpose Series—Gives men an in-depth look at real men from the Bible who provide poignant examples of godly masculinity by author and pastor Gene Getz.

Women of Purpose Series—Unique women's series blends interactive Bible study, experiences, and opportunities to connect with God, other women, and your own heart.

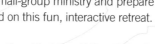

LEADERSHIP RESOURCES:

Churches world-wide have tapped into the experience and knowledge of Serendipity House by utilizing Leadership Resources to launch and develop dynamic small-group ministries.

Small-Group Kickoff Retreat: Experiential Training for Group Leaders
Jump start your small-group ministry and prepare your leaders to succeed on this fun, interactive retreat.

Great Beginnings: Your First Small-Group Study
Six interactive sessions are fun, easy, and perfect for developing a sense of connection in your group.

Ice-Breakers and Heart-Warmers
Provides a wealth of ideas for starting and ending all kinds of meetings.

Making the Critical Connection
Learn how to take the journey to transform Sunday School by incorporating the best of small-group dynamics.

Serendipity Bible for Groups
Our best-selling Bible over the years has over 30,000 small-group discussion questions that cover every passage of Scripture.

For these and other resources, visit www.SerendipityHouse.com.

INTRO

1 Juan Ramon Jimenez, "Heroic Reason" from *Selected Writings of Juan Ramon Jimenez*, (Farrar Straus Giroux, 1999)

SECTION 1:

2 Robert Frost, "The Road Not Taken," (The American Academy of Poets Web site: *http://www.poets.org/viewmedia.php/prmMID/15717*)

3 Donald Miller, *Searching for God Knows What*, (Thomas Nelson Publishers, 2004)

4 L. Frank Baum, *The Wonderful Wizard of Oz*, (Sterling; 2005)

5 John Eldredge, *Waking the Dead*, (Thomas Nelson Publishers, 2003)

6 Concept from Dan B, Allender, To Be Told, (Waterbrook Press, 2005)

7 Lyrics from "Where Everybody Knows Your Name" from LetsSingIt. com accessed from *http://artists.letssingit.com/phish-lyrics-where-everybody-knows-your-name-cheers-theme-nvk1z8n*, March 7, 2007.

SECTION 2:

8 Bill Donahue, *Leading Life-Changing Small Groups*, (Zondervan, 1996, p. 28)

9 Ken Blanchard, Patricia Zigarmi, and Drea Zigmari, *Leadership and the One Minute Manager®*, (HarperCollins Business, 2000)

10 Gene Wilkes, *Jesus on Leadership*, (Tyndale House Publishers, 1998)

11 Jim Collins, *Good to Great*, (HarperCollins, 2001)

SECTION 3:

12 Hal Mayer, *Making the Critical Connection*, (Serendipity House, 2005, pp. 9-10)

13 Donahue, Op. Cit. p. 28

SECTION 4:

14 Dave Buehring, *Cell Church Magazine*, "If I Could Do It All Over Again"

15 Randy Frazee, *Making Room for Life*, (Zondervan, 2004)

16 Henri Nouwen, Gracias: A Latin American Journal, (Orbis Books, 1993)

17 Joel Comiskey, *How to Lead a Great Cell Group Meeting So People Want to Come*, (Touch Publications, 2001)

18 Jay Firebaugh, Cell Church Magazine

19 Dr. Ralph W. Neighbour, Jr., *Cover the Bible*, (Touch Publications, 2002)

20 Richard J. Foster, *Prayer*, (Harper San Francisco, 1992)

21 John Franklin, *And the Place Was Shaken*, (B&H Publishing Group, 2005)

22 Franklin, op. cit.

23 Serendipity House, *Becoming Small Group Leaders* (Serendipity House, 2003)

SECTION 5:

24 Les Parrot, *How to Handle Impossible People, High-Maintenance Relationships*, (Tyndale, 1997)

DESTINATION:COMMUNITY

RICK **HOWERTON**

Meet Serendipity's "how-to" guy—Rick Howerton. He currently serves as the Director of Training and Events for Serendipity House and also as the pastor of a contemporary, small-group driven church—The Bridge. Rick is a veteran small-group specialist. A leader in small-group ministry for 20 years, Rick has been involved in the oversight of life-changing small groups on college campuses as well as in the local church, building one church's small-group ministry from nothing to 450 members in just a few short years. Rick speaks to thousands of small-group leaders across the country as he leads Serendipity House Small-Group Seminars and speaks at national conferences. For more information about Serendipity House conferences, visit *www.SerendipityHouse.com* on the Web.

Rick is a man of contagious passion. He has been on a journey from just knowing about Jesus to really knowing Jesus. The greatest passions in his life are Jesus, his family, his church, people, and equipping others to take the amazing adventure into doing life together in small groups

Rick resides near Nashville with his lovely wife, Julie. He has two incredible sons, Josh and Lee, and a wonderful daughter-in-law, Jana.